WHO IS GOETHE?

WHO IS GOETHE?

Edited by Katharina Mommsen

Translated by Leslie and Jeanne Willson

Suhrkamp Publishers, New York, Inc.

Library of Congress Cataloging in Publication Data
Goethe, Johann Wolfgang von, 1749–1832.
  Who is Goethe?
  I. Mommsen, Katharina, 1925–   . II. Title.
PT2026.A2M6 1983 831'6   82-10674
ISBN 3-518-03054-X

© Suhrkamp Publishers New York, Inc., 1983
Formerly ©Suhrkamp/Insel Publishers, Boston, 1983
ISBN 3-518-03054-X
Printed in USA

Photographs: Courtesy of Bayerische Staatsgemäldesammlungen, Neue Pinakothek, Munchen (Foto Kester/Bavaria Verlag)–10; Freies Deutsches Hochstift, Frankfurt am Main–1, 2, 3, 5, 8; Christoph Michel, Freiburg–4; Nationale Forschungs–und Gedenkstätten der klassischen deutschen Literatur in Weimar–6, 9, 11; Städelsches Kunstinstitut, Frankfurt am Main (Foto Ursula Edelmann)–7

Note: All translations are by Leslie and Jeanne Willson except where noted.

Preface

"Who is Goethe?" This question is as simple as it is complex, and even more so when we add that the person asked is a foreigner. WHO IS GOETHE? AIMEZ-VOUS GOETHE? CHI E GOETHE? QUIEN ES GOETHE? QUEM E GOETHE?

I asked Katharina Mommsen to prepare an Almanac with selections from Goethe for those who are little or scarcely or not at all acquainted with him. A collection of texts that show how ever-present Goethe is, that he has something to say to us today, that he is thoroughly "in" and "up to date." Katharina Mommsen has been teaching German literature at Stanford University in California for almost a decade; she knows her Geothe, on whom she has often worked, and she knows the young Americans who are interested in German, German culture and literature.

Katharina Mommsen has put together a collection of texts by Goethe, accompanied by documents and pictures. The core of the collection is composed of excerpts from his main works. Themes and characters are presented that are significant for today's reader. From *Werther* we read the passage concerning suicide and his criticism of society. Quotations from *Götz* and *Egmont* deal with the theme of freedom and also the figure of Klärchen and Egmont's love for a girl of the middle class. In *Wilhelm Meister* the role of woman is especially interesting to us today. In order to present an idea of the action in *Faust*, the editor focuses first on the relationship of Faust to Mephistopheles, the wager and its outcome; second, on the Gretchen tragedy and its ending. She then turns to the scene presenting Faust as a philanthropist, a friend of the people, which is related to the outcome of the wager in *Faust II*. These two scenes explain the "redemption."

In answer to the question "Who is Goethe?" information about Goethe's personality is certainly to be expected. Within the present limitations, the biographical material must concentrate on such facts as will be interesting to the reader in the area of politics and social affairs. The selection affords astonishing evidence of Goethe's beneficence and social effectiveness. Selections from the *Italian Journey* illuminate the most important experience in Goethe's life after the call to the Weimar court, and they also present Goethe, the scientist and ecologist.

In the passages collected here, in the poems, in the selections from prose works, essays, and dramas, a great arch is drawn from Frankfurt to Strassbourg to Weimar and into the world.

Who is Goethe? The reader of the passages in this collection will be able to answer that question for himself.

Siegfried Unseld

Goethe's Birth

August 28, 1749—Goethe is born
(From a letter written by Bettina Brentano to Goethe in 1810, repeating the story as Goethe's mother told it.)

"The bed upon which your mother brought you into this world had blue-checkered curtains. She was then eighteen years old and married for one year. You deliberated for three days before you came into the light of day, and you caused your mother hours of travail. Your grandmother stood at the end of the bed; when you first opened your eyes, she cried out: Elisabeth! He is alive! 'Then the heart of a mother was awakened within me, and it has remained since then in a constant state of enthusiasm up to this very hour,' she said to me in her seventy-fifth year. Your grandfather, who was a distinguished citizen and at that time a civil magistrate of the city, continually made use of chance and mischance to benefit the city, and so, too, your difficult birth became the incentive for the city to employ a doctor to deliver the babies of the poor. 'When still in the cradle, he was a blessing to mankind,' your mother told me."

My build from Father I inherit,
His neat and serious ways;
Combined with Mother's cheerful spirit,
Her love of telling stories.
Great-grandfather courted the loveliest,
His ghost won't leave me alone;
Great-grandmother liked fine jewels best,
This twitch I've also known.
If, then, no mortal chemist can
Divide the components from the whole,
What is there in the entire man
You could call original?

(Tame Xenias, IV, 1825)
Translated by Michael Hamburger

The house on Grosser Hirschgraben in Frankfurt, where Goethe was born.

KATHARINA MOMMSEN

Poems for Friederike Brion

In Strassburg, where Goethe received his law degree, he composed poems for Friederike Brion, a preacher's daughter from Sesenheim:

> Yet, to be loved, what happiness!
> What happiness, ye gods, to love!

(1771)
Translated by
Christopher Middleton

May Song

Marvellous Nature
Shining on me!
Glorious sunlight,
Field shaking with glee!

From all the branches
Flowerlets rush,
A thousand voices
Out of the bush,

And gladness, rapture
From every breast:
O sun, what pleasure!
O earth, how blest!

O love, with a golden
Glow you adorn
The hilltops yonder
Like mist in the morn,

Splendidly blessing
The meadow trim,
In a haze of blossom,
World full to the brim.

Sweetheart, I love you,
Your glances tell,
Sweet, how you love me,
Love me as well,

So does the lark love
Song and the blue,
And morning flowers
The heavenly dew,

So do I love you,
With hottest blood,
Who give me youth's gladness
And brace my mood

New songs to be making,
New dances to know:
Be happy for ever
In loving me so.

(1771)
Translated by
Christopher Middleton

KATHARINA MOMMSEN

Rosebud in the Heather

Urchin saw a rose—a dear
Rosebud in the heather.
Fresh as dawn and morning-clear;
Ran up quick and stooped to peer,
Took his fill of pleasure,
Rosebud, rosebud, rosebud red,
Rosebud in the heather.

Urchin blurts: "I'll pick you, though,
Rosebud in the heather!"
Rosebud: "Then I'll stick you so
That there's no forgetting, no!
I'll not stand it, ever!"
Rosebud, rosebud, rosebud red,
Rosebud in the heather.

But the wild young fellow's torn
Rosebud from the heather.
Rose, she pricks him with her thorn;
Should she plead, or cry forlorn?
Makes no difference whether.
Rosebud, rosebud, rosebud red,
Rosebud in the heather.

(1771)
Translated by J.F. Nims

Johann Caspar Goethe (1710-1782): lawyer and imperial councillor. Pastel drawing by Hermann Junker from a relief by J.P. Melchior of 1779.

KATHARINA MOMMSEN

Catharina Elisabeth Goethe (1731-1808): daughter of the mayor of Frankfurt, Johann Wolfgang Textor. Pastel drawing by Georg Oswald May, 1776.

WHO IS GOETHE?

Farewell to Friederike

After leaving Friederike: sorrow about the state she is in.

Friederike's answer to my written farewell tore at my heart. It was the same hand, the same mind, the same feeling that had been cultivated by me and for me. Now for the first time I felt the loss that she suffered and saw no possibility of making up for it or even easing it. She was always present in my mind; constantly I was aware that she was missing, and the worst was that I could not forgive my own distress. They had taken Gretchen from me, Annette had left me, now for the first time I was to blame; I had wounded to the depths the fairest heart, and so this epoch was one of dismal remorse, in the absence of an accustomed, comforting love, painful in the extreme, even unbearable. But a person must live, so I took a sincere interest in others, I sought to disentangle them from their perplexities and to unite those who were about to part, so that they might not fare as I had. . .

At a time when my grief over Friederike's state filled me with anxiety, once more in my accustomed way I sought relief through my poetry. I resumed my customary poetical confessions in order to become worthy of an inner absolution through this self-tormenting penitence. The two Marias in *Götz von Berlichingen* and *Clavigo* and the two base characters who play their lovers may well have been the result of such penitent reflection.

(Truth and Poetry, Book 12)

KATHARINA MOMMSEN

The New Melusine

His most important poetical confession is not mentioned here: the Gretchen tragedy in *Faust*, which originated at that time. An explanation of the separation from Friederike is conveyed by Goethe by way of suggestion in the Sesenheim segment of his auto-biography, through an allusion to his fairy tale "The New Melusine." The hero loves and marries the daughter of the king of the dwarves but is unable to endure the life of a dwarf among dwarves for long:

Everything around me was completely suitable to my present shape and my needs, the bottles and mugs well proportioned for a small drinker, even, if you like, a comparatively better size than with us. To my little palate the delicate morsels tasted excellent, a kiss from the little mouth of my wife was only too charming, and I will not deny that the novelty made all these circumstances very pleasant for me. But unfortunately I had still not forgotten my former condition. I felt within me the standards of my former size that made me uneasy and unhappy. Now I understood for the first time what the philosophers must mean by their Ideals that men are supposed to be so tormented by. I had an Ideal of myself, and in my dreams I often seemed to myself to be a giant. Suffice it to say, my wife, the ring, my dwarf's shape, so many other bonds made me altogether unhappy, so that I began to think seriously of my liberation.

Because I was convinced that all the magic lay concealed in the ring, I determined to file it off.

(*Wilhelm Meister's Journeyman Years*
Volume 3, Chapter 6)

His first novel brings the twenty-five-year-old Goethe the greatest success of his life. It reflects the sentiments of a new generation and a new era.

The Sufferings of Young Werther

Conversation with Albert about Suicide

[Albert] "I cannot imagine how a person could be so foolish as to shoot himself; the mere thought disgusts me."

"That you people," I exclaimed, "in order to talk about a subject, must say right off: That is foolish, that is smart, that is good, that is bad! And what is that all supposed to mean? Have you thus explored the inner circumstances of a deed? Do you know with certainty how to explain the causes, why they happened, why they had to happen? If you had done that, you would not be so hasty with your judgments."

"You will grant me," said Albert, "that certain actions are still wicked, no matter what the motive for them might have been."

I shrugged my shoulders and conceded that. "Still, dear friend," I continued, "even here there are a few exceptions. It is true that theft is wicked; but the man who goes out to commit robbery in order to save himself and his own from actual starvation, does he deserve pity or punishment? Who will raise the first stone against a husband who in righteous anger destroys his unfaithful wife and her base seducer? Or against the girl who in one blissful hour loses herself in the irresistible joy of love? Our laws themselves, cold-blooded and pedantic, can be moved to suspend their punishment."

"That is something quite different," Albert replied, "because someone who is carried away by his passions loses all power of reason and, like a drunkard, is regarded as insane."

"Oh you sensible people!" I smilingly exclaimed. "Passion! Drunkenness! Insanity! You stand there so composed, so uninvolved, you moral people! Reproach the drinker, detest the insane person, pass by like the priest and thank God like the Pharisee that He did not make you like one of these. I have been drunk more than once, my emotions were never far from madness, and I do not repent of either; for I have learned to understand in my fashion how all

KATHARINA MOMMSEN

extraordinary men, who accomplished something great, something seemingly impossible, were from time immemorial always cried down as drunkards and madmen.

"But even in everyday life it is unbearable to hear called after almost every single person engaged in an even halfway free, noble, unexpected deed: 'The man is drunk, he is crazy!' Shame on you, you sober people! Shame on you, you wise men!"

"Now that is one of your odd notions again," said Albert, "you exaggerate everything and are certainly incorrect, at least here, when you compare suicide, about which we are now speaking, with great actions, since it cannot really be considered anything else but a weakness. For it is certainly easier to die than to bear resolutely a life full of anguish."

I was on the point of breaking off; for no argument upsets me more than someone who cites an inconsequential common expression when I am speaking with my whole heart. But I controlled myself because I had already heard that so often and more often been annoyed by it, and I rejoined with vigor: "You call that weakness? I beg you, do not be deceived by appearances. A people who groan under the unbearable yoke of a tyrant, do you dare to call that weak when they finally become aroused and break their chains; a person who, alarmed because his house has caught fire, finds his strength totally engaged and carries off burdens with ease that he can scarcely move when his mind is calm; one who in a rage over an insult takes on six others and overpowers them, are they to be called weak? And, my good fellow, if struggle is strength, why should overexcitement be the opposite?"

Albert looked at me and said: "Don't think ill of me, the examples that you are presenting do not seem to belong here at all."

"It may be," I said, "I have often been reproached by the fact that my way of thinking often borders on the fustian. Let us see then if we can demonstrate in a different way how a person must feel, who decides to cast away what is usually the pleasant burden of life. For only insofar as we can feel compassion do we have the right to speak on a subject.

"Human nature," I continued, "has its limits: It can tolerate joy, suffering, pain, up to a certain degree and perishes as soon as that is exceeded. So the question here is not whether one is strong or weak but rather whether one can survive the extent of one's suffering, be it moral or physical; and I consider it just as strange to say that a man is cowardly, who takes his own life, as it would be impertinent to call a person a coward who dies of a virulent fever."

"Paradoxical! Very paradoxical!" Albert exclaimed.

"Not so much as you think," I replied. "You will grant me that we call it a mortal illness when one's constitution is so weakened, one's strength partly consumed, partly put out of operation, so that it cannot help itself again and is incapable of reestablishing the usual course of life through some happy radical change.

"Now, dear friend, let us apply that to the mind. Look at a man in his limitations, how impressions affect him, how ideas gain a foothold with him until finally a growing passion robs him of all his tranquil strength of mind and destroys him.

"In vain does the calm, reasonable man survey the condition of an unhappy person; in vain does he reassure him! It is the same as a healthy man who stands by the bed of a sick one and cannot instil in him the slightest bit of his strength."

For Albert that was expressed too generally. I reminded him of a girl who had been found dead in the water a short time ago and repeated her story to him.— A good, young creature, who had grown up in a narrow circle of domestic occupation, of weekly, appointed work, who knew no other prospect of amusement than perhaps to promenade around the city on Sunday in gradually acquired finery with those like herself, perhaps to dance a bit on all the special holidays, and otherwise with all the liveliness of the most hearty participation to chatter away many an hour with a neighbor girl about the reason for some squabble or a piece of scandal. Her fiery nature then finally feels more fervent needs that are enhanced by the flattery of men; her erstwhile pleasures gradually become uninteresting until she finally meets a man on whom she then casts all her hopes, forgets the world around her, hears nothing, sees nothing, feels nothing but him, the only one, yearns for him alone, the only one. Never spoiled by the empty diversion of fickle vanity, she is drawn by her desire straight to her goal; she wants to be his, she wants to find in everlasting union all the happiness that she lacks, to enjoy the union of all the pleasures for which she longs. Repeated promises that seal for her the assurance of all her hopes, daring caresses that increase her desires, encircle her whole soul; she hovers in a vague consciousness, in anticipation of all joys, she is exceedingly tense. Finally she stretches out her arms to embrace all her desires—and her lover forsakes her. Benumbed, without feeling, she stands before an abyss; all is darkness around her, no expectations, no solace, no hope, for he in whom alone she perceived her existence has left her. She does not see the wide world that lies before her, not the many who could replace her loss; she feels alone, abandoned by all the world—and blindly, crowded into a corner by the awful misery of her heart, she hurls herself down in order to smother all her agony in the encirclement of death.—"See, Albert, that is the story of so many human beings! And tell me, is that not the case with sickness? The constitution can find no way out of the labyrinth of bewildering and conflicting forces, and the man must die.

"Woe betide him who could look on and say: 'The fool! If she had waited, if she had let time take its effect, her despair would have ceased and another would certainly have been found to comfort her!' That is just as if one said: 'The fool has died of a fever! If he had only waited until his strength had returned, his bodily fluids had improved, the disturbance to his circulation had ceased, all would have gone well, and he would be alive today.' "

Albert, to whom the comparison was still not evident, continued to object somewhat, among other things that I had spoken only of a simple girl; how a man of intelligence who was not so limited, who was aware of more situations, might be excused, he could not comprehend.

"My friend," I exclaimed, "a man is a man, and the small amount of intelligence that one may have counts for little or not at all when passion rages and the limits of human nature close in on one. Rather—About that another time," I said and grabbed for my hat. Oh, my heart was so full—And we parted without having understood one another. Just as no one in this world can easily understand another.

(Book 1, August 12)

Political Interest: The Model of America

Political interests that are today also of primary interest to the new generation govern Goethe's thinking. Freedom and social change are demanded. The model is America and its Revolution.

But the interest of the world became even more spiritedly engaged when a whole people threatened to set themselves free. At an earlier time the same drama, only smaller, had been watched with pleasure; Corsica had for a long time been the place toward which all eyes turned; when Paoli, not able to carry out his patriotic plan any further, traveled through Germany to England, he drew all hearts to him; he was a fair, slim, blond man, filled with charm and friendliness; I saw him at the Bethmanns' house, where he stayed for a short time and treated the curious who crowded around him with serene kindness. But now similar events were said to be recurring in that more distant part of the world; everyone wished the Americans all good luck, and the names of Franklin and Washington began to glitter and glisten on the political and martial horizon. Much had happened for the relief of mankind . . . and youth in its confidence believed it might promise a fine, even glorious, future for itself and its contemporaries.

(*Truth and Poetry*, Book 17)

It cannot be concealed that after the Hubertusburg Treaty [1763] . . . the Germans were searching for something else, and a certain vague inclination, if not for something better, certainly for something different gradually developed in them. The Third Estate improved progressively; the better noblemen, who had confidence in themselves, did not want to fall behind and joined with them;

KATHARINA MOMMSEN

the others, who relied on their privileges, treated the Third Estate with aversion, with contempt, especially the women.

After the sympathy that was given to Corsica and then to America, this
interest became more intimate.

(*Campaign in France*,
Draft of an Introduction)

The fight for political freedom is the theme of the first great dramas, *Götz von Berlichingen* and *Egmont*. Consciously Goethe fights against "contempt toward women," especially in *Egmont*. This work marks the prelude to the esteem of women in all Goethe's later writing.

Götz von Berlichingen
Act 3: *Long live freedom*

GOTTFRIED:
That shall be our last word but one, when we die.

GEORG:
Long live freedom!

ALL:
Long live freedom!

GOTTFRIED:
And when this lives after us, we can die in peace. For we can see in our imagination our grandchildren happy and the emperor of our grandchildren happy.

If the servants of the princes serve them as nobly and freely as you serve me, if the princes serve the emperor as I would like to serve him.

GEORG:
Then many things must change.

GOTTFRIED:
They will! They will! Perhaps God will open the eyes of the great to their happiness. I hope so, for their delusion is so unnatural that no miracle seems necessary for their enlightenment. If they will feel the abundancy of joy to be happy in their subjects. If they will have human enough hearts to savor the bliss it is to be a great man.

If the round cheeks, the cheerful appearance of every peasant, his numerous family, puts the seal to the abundance of their peaceful land, and in the presence of this sight all plays, all galleries of paintings become cold for them. Then neighbor will grant neighbor peace, because he is happy himself. Then no one will seek to expand his borders. He will prefer to re-

KATHARINA MOMMSEN

main the sun in its orbit, rather than as a comet press his frightful, inconstant passage through many others.

GEORG:

And we would ride after him.

GOTTFRIED:

I dare say God would that Germany were at this moment so. We would clear the mountains of wolves, would fetch a roast from the woods for our neighbor, peacefully tilling the soil, and in return eat soup with him. . . That would be a life, if a person would risk his own skin for the sake of the common good.

Egmont

Egmont's beloved: a simple commoner

MOTHER (*crying*):

Go on and cry! make me more miserable with your distress! Is it not trouble enough that my only daughter is a ruined creature?

CLARA (*rising, and coldly*):

Ruined! Egmont's beloved ruined?—What princess is there who does not envy poor, little Clara her place in his heart! O Mother—my Mother, you never spoke like this before. Dear Mother, be kind!—People, what they think, the neighbors, what they whisper.—This room, this little house is heaven, since Egmont's love dwells within it.

MOTHER:

One has to like him! that is true. He is always so friendly, free, and open.

CLARA:

There is not a mean bone in him. You see, Mother, and still he is the great Egmont. And when he comes to me, how dear he is, how good! how gladly he would conceal his position, his gallantry, from me! how concerned he is about me! such a human being, such a friend, such a beloved.

MOTHER:

Will he come today?

CLARA:
Haven't you seen how often I have gone to the window? Haven't you noticed how heedful I was of any noise at the door? Even though I know that he will not come before night, still I expect him every moment from morning on, when I arise. If I were only a boy and could always go with him, to court and everywhere! If only I could bear the flag behind him into battle!

MOTHER:
You were always such a harum-scarum child; even when you were small, now wild, now pensive. Won't you dress up a little nicer?

CLARA:
Perhaps, Mother! If I am bored—Yesterday, just think, some of his people passed by and sang songs of praise about him. At least his name was in the songs, I could not understand the rest. My heart was in my throat—I would have liked to call them back, if I had not been ashamed.

MOTHER:
Take care! Your impetuous nature will spoil everything; you will expose yourself plainly to those people.

(Act I, Scene 3, Commoner's house)

The Repression of Freedom among the People

EGMONT:
. . . The Lowlanders fear a double yoke, and who will vouch for their freedom?

ALBA:
Freedom! A pretty word for those who understand it right. What kind of freedom do they want? What is the freedom of those most free?—To do the right!—and the King will not prohibit them from that. No! no! they think they are not free when they cannot harm themselves and others. Would it not be better to abdicate than to rule such a people? When foreign enemies, of whom no citizen is aware who is concerned only with what is close by, press near, then they disagree among themselves and they almost conspire with their enemies. It is far better to limit them so that they are kept like children, that they can be guided like children to their own good. Believe me, a people does not grow old, nor smart, a people remains forever childlike.

                                                KATHARINA MOMMSEN

EGMONT:

How seldom a king comes to his senses. And should the many not rely rather on many but on one, and not even on the one but on the few of that one, on the people who grow old under the eyes of their master. I suppose they alone have the right to become smart.

ALBA:

Perhaps for just that reason that they are not left to their own devices.

EGMONT:

And for that reason do not want to leave anyone else to his own devices. Do whatever you will—I have given my answer to your questions and repeat it: It will not work! It cannot work! I know my fellow countrymen. They are men worthy to tread upon God's earth, each one plainly for himself a little king, firm, energetic, capable, true, attached to old customs. It is hard to earn their trust, easy to keep it. Inflexible and firm! They can be oppressed but not suppressed.

ALBA (*who has meanwhile looked around several times*):

Could you repeat all that in the presence of the King?

EGMONT:

So much the worse, if his presence intimidated me! So much the better for him, for his people, if he gives me the courage, if he fills me with the confidence to say far more.

ALBA:

What is useful I can hear as he can.

EGMONT:

I would say to him: The shepherd can easily drive a whole herd of sheep before him, the ox pulls his plow without resistance; but you must learn the thoughts of the noble horse, if you will ride it, you must do nothing unwise, require nothing unwise from it. And so the common folk wish to retain their old system of government, to be ruled over by their fellow countrymen, because they know how they will be led, because they can expect unselfishness from them, and interest in their destiny.

ALBA:

But should the sovereign not have the authority to change these old traditions, should not just this be his first privilege? What is there permanent upon this earth? So should a system of government be able to endure? Will

not every circumstance be altered in the flow of time and just for this reason
an old system of government become the source of a thousand evils because
it does not comprehend the current condition of the people? I fear that these
old rights are so agreeable because they create hiding places where the
shrewd and powerful can conceal themselves or sneak through to the dis-
advantage of the people, to the harm of the whole populace.

EGMONT:
And these arbitrary changes, this uncontrolled intervention by the highest
power, are they not indications that one person wants to do what thousands
could not do? He wants to make himself alone free to be able to satisfy his
every wish, to realize his every thought. And if we trust him completely, a
good, wise king, is he responsible for his successors? that not one will rule
without discretion, without forbearance? Who will save us then from complete despotism, if he sends us his servants, those nearest to him, who
without knowledge of the land and its needs conduct themselves as they
please, find no opposition, and know themselves to be free of every respon-
sibility?

ALBA (*who has looked around again meanwhile*):
There is nothing more natural than that a king should plan to rule by
himself and prefer to charge those with his commands who wish to understand him, who will execute his will unquestioningly.

EGMONT:
And it is just as natural that the common man wishes to be governed by one
who was born and raised with him, who has the same concept as he of just
and unjust, whom he can think of as his brother.

ALBA:
And yet the nobleman has shared very unequally with these, his brothers.

EGMONT:
That happened centuries ago and now is tolerated without envy. If,
however, new men were sent unnecessarily, who aimed to enrich themselves
for the second time at the expense of the nation, if they should see
themselves exposed to a harsh, audacious, absolute greed, that would create
an upheaval that would not easily resolve itself.

ALBA:
You tell me what I should not listen to. I, too, am foreign here.

KATHARINA MOMMSEN

EGMONT:

The fact that I am telling you should show you that I do not mean you.

ALBA:

But even so, I did not wish to hear it from you. The King dispatched me with the hope that I would find support among the nobles here. The King *will* have his way. The King has seen, after profound deliberation, what will benefit the people; things cannot continue and remain as before. The King's intention is: for their own good, to limit them, to press upon them their own welfare, if it must be, to sacrifice destructive citizens so that the others will find their peace and can enjoy the fortune of a wise government. This is his resolve, and I have orders to notify the nobles of it, and in his name I ask advice on *how* to do it, not *what*, for he has determined that.

EGMONT:

I am afraid your words justify the fear of the people, the common fear! So he has then determined what no prince should determine. The power of the people, their soul, the concept of themselves that they hold, he means to weaken, to depress, to destroy, in order easily to rule them. He will corrupt the inner core of their individuality, assuredly with the intention of making them happier. He will destroy them, so that they can become something, a different something. Oh, if his intention is good, he is still misled! The opposition is not to the King, they only stand in the way of the King, who, traveling on a treacherous road, takes the first unhappy step.

Meeting with Duke Carl August
of Sachsen-Weimar

The young Goethe was searching for an occupation in which he could be effective in regard to his political ideas. There were a few courts in Germany where the sovereign and the nobility were progressively inclined and interested in both art and science. He knew of one in Weimar, where a famous poet—Wieland—had already taken up residence. Carl August, who would be the next duke of Weimar, became interested in Goethe as the author of *Götz von Berlichingen* and of *Werther*. At their first meeting (1774) their conversation about the statesman and historian Justus Möser became the underlying reason that Goethe later became a minister of state in Weimar. But in his old age Goethe said about Möser that he "would know of no one to compare him with except Benjamin Franklin" [*Truth and Poetry*, Book 13, conclusion]. Goethe gives an account in his autobiography.

Once a slim, handsome man came to visit me. . . . He said his name was Knebel. . . . Scarcely had we finished discussing subjects that concerned German literature in general, when I discovered to my satisfaction that he was currently . . . employed in Weimar. I had already heard many favorable things about conditions there; for many strangers came to visit us from there, who had witnessed how the Duchess Amalia was calling together the most superior men for the education of her prince; how the Academy at Jena had contributed its part to this fine objective with its important teachers, how the arts were not only protected by the aforementioned duchess but even thoroughly and zealously promoted by her. Also, it was understood that Wieland was held in particular favor and that the *Deutsche Merkur*, which collected the works of so many foreign scholars, contributed not a little to the reputation of the city where it was published. One of the best German theaters was established there

KATHARINA MOMMSEN

and was famous because of the actors as well as the authors who worked for it. ... Now as I inquired about these persons and things, as if I were an old acquaintance, and expressed the desire to become more familiar with the circumstances there, the newcomer replied in a very friendly way: Nothing could be easier than that, for the crown prince [Carl August] and his brother Prince Constantine had just arrived in Frankfurt and were desirous of talking to me and getting to know me. I immediately showed the greatest willingness to call on him, and my new friend answered that I should not delay, because their sojourn would not last long. Preparatory to doing this, I took him to my parents, who were very surprised at his arrival and message and conversed with him with pleasure. Then I hurried off with him to the young princes, who received me in an open and friendly way. . . . Although there was immediately no lack of literary conversation between us, still a chance occurrence provided the best beginning, so that ours might be a meaningful and fruitful conversation.

There lay on the table a copy of Möser's *Patriotic Fantasies* and, in fact, the first part, freshly bound and uncut. Since I knew it very well but the other parties knew it only slightly, I had the advantage of being able to deliver a detailed account of it; and this turned out to be the most appropriate start for a conversation with a young prince who had the best intentions and the firmest resolution to really effect good from his position. Möser's presentation, both in regard to the content as well as the sense, could not help but be extremely interesting to every German. Although the German Empire is as a rule reproached for its disunity, anarchy, and impotence, from Möser's standpoint it was precisely this multitude of little states that appeared highly desirable for the spread of culture in the individual ones, according to the requirements that arise from the character and condition of the most varied provinces. . . .

At dinner this conversation was continued, and it inspired a better opinion of me than I perhaps deserved. For, instead of making those works that I myself was capable of producing the subject of the conversation and claiming undivided attention for the drama or the novel, in Möser I appeared rather to give preference to the kind of writer whose talent proceeded from an active life and, immediately useful, forthwith returned to the same again, while real poetic works that soar over the moral and the physical areas can only be of use in a roundabout way and then almost only by chance. These conversations were like the fairy tale of *The Thousand and One Nights*: One important subject slid in and over the other, many themes were only slightly touched without the possibility of pursuing them; and so, because the sojourn of the young noblemen could be only of short duration in Frankfurt, the promise, which I gladly made, was obtained from me that I should follow them to Mainz and there spend a few days, and I hurried home with this cheerful news to tell it to my parents.

However, my father was not about to consent to this at all; for following his views as a member of the German middle class, he had always kept at a distance from the nobility . . . indeed, the courts belonged to those objects about which he was accustomed to joke, and he even welcomed it when he was opposed somewhat; one must only, according to his opinion, behave wittily and cleverly in doing so. . . .

Through all such rejoinders my father could not be diverted from his views, however. . . . He warned me unyieldingly and maintained the invitation was just to lure me into a trap. . . . However much I was convinced now of the opposite, in that I saw only too clearly that a preconceived opinion aroused by melancholy illusions made the estimable man anxious, nevertheless I did not just want to act directly against his convictions, and still I could not find some pretext through which I could take back my promise again without appearing thankless and rude. . . . [Finally I succeeded] in obtaining the permission of my father, who gave in, although suspiciously and reluctantly.

So I arrived at the specified time in a very cold season in Mainz and was received in a very friendly way by the young noblemen and their companions, in accordance with the invitation. We recalled the discussion in Frankfurt, what we had begun we continued. . . . The few days of my stay in Mainz passed very pleasantly; for when my new patrons were kept away from the house by social calls and dinner parties, I stayed with their household, painted some of them, and also even went skating, for which the frozen fortress moats provided the best opportunity. Full of the kindness that I had met there, I returned home.

. . . My father, instead of being happy about the favorable conclusion of this little adventure, persevered in his opinion and maintained that this was all only pretense on their part and perhaps they had it in mind to carry out something

KATHARINA MOMMSEN

more unpleasant toward me in the future. Thus I was compelled to take my story to my younger friends, to whom I really could not relate the affair in enough detail. . .

Everything pointed to an invigoratingly active literary and artistic life. And so gradually that element became clear, on which the young duke was to have an effect after his return. . . . The mine at Ilmenau, which had come to a standstill, for which a possible resumption could be insured by an expensive support of the deep tunnel, the Academy at Jena [University of Jena], which had fallen somewhat behind the spirit of the times and was threatened with the loss of precisely its most capable teachers, and so much besides, aroused a high-minded public spirit. They looked around for individuals who could be called upon to demand such diverse good things in Germany, as it struggled upwards, and so a completely fresh prospect emerged, such as an energetic and spirited youth could ever wish for.

(Truth and Poetry
Books 15 and 20)

Lili Schönemann

At Easter in 1775 Goethe became engaged to Lili Schönemann (1758-1817), the daughter of a Frankfurt banker. But neither the life style nor the religious persuasion of the two families was compatible. In addition, the Schönemanns urged their daughter to make a rich match, by which their banking house—which was on the verge of bankruptcy— could be revitalized. In the fall the engagement was broken. Goethe went to Weimar. In 1778 Lili married a Strassburg banker, the Baron of Türkheim.

A New Love, a New Life

Heart, my heart, what is this change now?
What oppresses you this way?
What a life so new and strange now!
Who you are I cannot say.
Everything you loved has vanished,
All your grievances you've banished—
Oh, what led you to surcease
Of all your industry and peace!

Does the bloom of youth enfold you
In this dear, enchanting shape,
Eyes with faith and goodness hold you,
From whose power there's no escape?
If I choose these ties to sever,
Bravely hope to flee her ever,
In that moment, though I've tried,
My way leads back to her side.

With this thread, enchantment laden,
That I cannot sever still,
Holds this dear, disheveled maiden
Me so firm against my will.
Must I truly now endeavor
In her spell to live forever?
Oh, how great the change would be!
Love, O love, please set me free!

(1775)

Anna Elisabeth (Lili) Schönemann (1758-1817); 1778 married Turckheim. Pastel drawing by F.B. Frey, 1782.

A Lili Anecdote: The "Brush Off"

Among Lili's most charming peculiarities was one that can be expressed here by the word and gesture as a "brush off," and which took place when something objectionable was said or spoken, especially when at the dinner table or in the vicinity of a flat surface. This had its origin in an immensely charming naughty trick that she once committed when a stranger, who was sitting next to her at the table, brought up something improper. Without changing her pleasant expression, she brushed her right hand quite charmingly across the tablecloth and deliberately shoved everything she could reach with this gentle motion onto the floor. I do not know what all—knives, forks, bread, the salt shaker, even something there for the use of her neighbor. Everyone was startled; the servants came running, no one knew what it was about except those who were aware that she was retaliating for unseemly conduct and effacing it in such an elegant way.

So here a symbol was originated for the rejection of something offensive that is, after all, in the habit of occurring often in good, upright, estimable, but not completely well-bred company. We all took the liberty to use the gesture with the right hand as a rejection; the actual sweeping away of objects she allowed herself only with restraint and taste.

(*Truth and Poetry*, Book 17)

 KATHARINA MOMMSEN

Lili Ready to Emigrate to America with Goethe!

I did not avoid and could not avoid seeing Lili; there was a tender, sensitive state between the two of us. I was advised that in my absence [a trip to Switzerland] she had been fully convinced that she must part from me. . . . Those who wished me well had confided to me that Lili had remarked, when all the obstacles to our alliance were recited to her: She would certainly venture, because of her feelings for me, to abandon all present affairs and relations and go with me to America. America was at that time perhaps even more than Eldorado is now to those who found themselves troubled by a situation like her present one.

(Truth and Poetry, Book 19)

Parting from Lili–Departure for Weimar

I had renounced all claims to Lili with conviction, but love made this conviction questionable to me. Lili had parted from me in the same way, and I had set out on that lovely, distracting journey [to Switzerland in 1775]; but it produced exactly the opposite effect.

As long as I was gone, I believed that we were apart but not permanently separated. All my memories, hopes, desires had free play. Then I returned, and as the reunion of free and happy lovers is a paradise, so is a reunion of two persons, separated only for practical reasons, an intolerable purgatory, an anteroom to Hell. When I returned to Lili's company, I felt doubly all those differences that our relationship had disturbed; when I again entered into her presence, it oppressed me that she was lost for me.

For that reason I decided once more on flight, and so nothing could be more desirable than that the young, ducal pair from Weimar should come from Karlsruhe to Frankfurt and I, in consequence of earlier and later invitations, should follow them to Weimar.

(Truth and Poetry, Book 20)

KATHARINA MOMMSEN

"Doctor Goethe" in Weimar

Goethe moved to Weimar in the year 1775. This young, fiery, twenty-six-year-old doctor—for he was called that at the time—generated a wonderful revolution in this place, which had been rather uncultured and now had suddenly become gifted with genius. It was no wonder. No more attractive man can be imagined. Considering his spirited intellect and his energy, the most unusual combination of mental and physical perfection, big, strong, and handsome; in all physical sports—riding, fencing, jumping, dancing—he was the first. . . . In addition to all that, there was also his favor with the young duke, who had just begun his reign and whom he had also suddenly snatched away from a pedantic, narrow, pampered court existence into a free life and so set about getting him to take ice-cold baths in the winter, kept him constantly in the open air, and rode around with him through his country, in the course of which there was much good carousing everywhere; but in this way they also acquired a thorough knowledge of the country and its individuals. The first natural result of this heroic cure was, to be sure, a dangerous illness of the duke, but he fortunately survived, and the result was a body hardened for the rest of his life, so that he could endure enormous fatigue. —Enough of that, a complete upheaval followed. All the young people put on Goethe's uniform, a yellow vest and knee pants and a dark-blue coat, and played Werther; the old folks grumbled and groaned. Everything was going to rack and ruin.

(Christoph W. Hufeland
Autobiography)

Johann Wolfgang Goethe. Oil painting by Georg Melchior Kraus, Weimar 1775/76.

                                                      KATHARINA MOMMSEN

Goethe Talks about Duke Carl August

He was eighteen when I came to Weimar, but by that time the buds and shoots on the tree were already indicating what it would one day be like. He soon attached himself most intimately to me and took a profound interest in everything that I did. The fact that I was almost ten years older than he was good for our relationship. He sat with me through whole evenings in deep conversation about matters concerning art and nature and whatever other diverse good subjects presented themselves. We often sat up until late at night, and it was not infrequent that we fell asleep next to one another on my sofa. For fifty years we went on in this way together; and it would be no wonder, if we finally accomplished something by it. . .

He was a man of the whole and for him everything came from one single great source. And as the whole was good, so also were the parts, let him do and work at whatever he would. Furthermore, three things were especially useful to him in the management of power. He had the gift of discerning men of intelligence and of character and of putting each one in his place. . . . He was inspired by the greatest good will, by the purest love for his fellow man, and with his whole heart he wanted only the best. He always thought first of the prosperity of his country and at the very last only a little of himself. His hand was always ready and open to meet high-minded men, to help promote good objectives. . . . He would have liked to make all mankind happy. But love engenders love. One who is loved can rule with ease. . . . He was greater than his surroundings. Next to ten voices that reached his ear concerning some certain case, he perceived the eleventh, better one in himself. He paid no heed to insinuations, and he did not easily get into a situation of doing something unprincely by turning against those whose merits had been put in question and by taking into his protection the rascals who had been recommended. He observed everything himself, judged everything himself, and in every case had his most secure foundation in himself. At the same time he had a reserved nature, and his deeds conformed to his words.

(To Eckermann *Conversations with Goethe*
October 23, 1828)

KATHARINA MOMMSEN

Goethe in Service to the State of Weimar
A letter of Duke Carl August to the
Opposition to Goethe's Appointment

My privy councillor, I have duly received your letter of April 24th. In it you express to me your opinion in all sincerity, as I expected from such an upright man as you are. You demand in the same that you be discharged from office because, you say: *You can no longer sit on a board of which Dr. Goethe is a member.*

This should really not be sufficient cause to make you form this resolve. If Dr. Goethe were a man of doubtful character, everyone would approve of your decision, but Goethe is an upright man with an extremely good and sensible heart; not I alone, but discerning men wish me luck in acquiring this man. His ability and genius are well known. You will realize yourself that a man like this could not endure the boredom and mechanical work of rising from the ranks on a provincial council. Not to use a man of genius in a place where he can use his extraordinary talents means: To misuse the same. I hope you are convinced of this truth just as I am. . .

Concerning the opinion of the world that might disapprove of my putting Dr. Goethe on my most important council without him first being either magistrate, professor, councillor of the exchequer or privy councillor: This changes nothing at all! The world passes judgment according to its prejudices, but I and everyone who wants to do his duty does not work to achieve fame but to be able to justify himself before God and his own conscience and tries to act also without the approval of the world.

After all this, I am certainly very surprised that you, my privy councillor, form the determination to leave me now at a moment when you yourself must, and certainly do, feel how much I need you. How very distasteful it cannot help but be to me, that you, instead of making it a pleasure to cultivate a young, capable man, as the frequently mentioned Dr. Goethe is, through your experience acquired in faithful service of twenty-two years, intend rather to leave my service and in a way that is offensive to Dr. Goethe as well as—I cannot deny it—to me! For it seems as if it were a disgrace for you to sit on the same board with him whom I, after all, as is known to you, look upon as my friend and who has never given occasion that he should be scorned but rather deserves the love of all upright people.

(To the president of the Privy Council,
J.F. von Fritsch, May 10, 1776)

KATHARINA MOMMSEN

The Charisma and Social Action of Goethe As Observed by his Contemporaries

If Goethe is ever happy in this world, then he will make thousands happy; and if he never is, then he will remain a meteor at which our contemporaries will stare themselves tired and our children warm themselves.

(J.G. Schlosser, 1773)

A woman of the world, who saw him frequently, tells me that Goethe was the most handsome man, the most vital, the most original, the most ardent, the most impetuous, the sweetest, the most seductive, and the most *dangerous* to the *heart* of a woman whom she has seen in her life.

My friend Lavater wrote me from Frankfurt on June 23, 1774: . . . "You would idolize Doctor Goethe. He is the most *formidable* and the most *charming* man."

(Joh. Georg Zimmermann to Charlotte von Stein
January 19, 1775)

I became acquainted with Goethe. That was the first happy hour of my youth. He offered me his help. I didn't tell him everything and just left, because I would rather die than accept something I had not earned. . . . That grand Goethe urged me strongly, remonstrated with me, and now I have lived for a whole year on his kindness.

(Klinger to Lenz, 1775)

Goethe was never a benefactor of mine other than on the part of heart and mind. All the help that he offered me I have not accepted.

(Lenz, Sketch, 1775)

For nine weeks now I have lived with Goethe and live . . . totally in *him*. He is in all respects and from all aspects the greatest, best, most magnificent human creature that God has created. Today there was one hour in which I saw him for the first time in his full magnificence—his completely beautiful, sensitive, pure humanity. Losing all self-control I kneeled down beside him, pressed my heart on his breast, and thanked God.

(Wieland, 1773-1813, to J.G. Zimmermann
January 8, 1776)

[In the spring of 1776 Stilling was completely destitute, could not pay his rent. Goethe sent him a letter with] *a hundred and fifteen Reichstalers in gold.* With astonishment he opened the letter, read it—and discovered that his friend Goethe, without his knowledge, had had the beginning of his story with the title "Stilling's Youth" printed, and here was the honorarium. . . . Then he and his wife embraced each other, wept loudly, and praised God. During Stilling's last trip to Frankfurt Goethe had received the famous call to Weimar and had furthered the publishing of Stilling's story there.

(Heinrich Stilling's Domestic Life)

Concerning poorhouses; Goethe made experiments at his own expense in Weimar, with which he was satisfied.

(J.A. Leisewitz' Journal, 1780)

1783, February 5-7. Goethe's servant Chr. Sutor gives an account to Eckermann:

"Once he [Goethe] rang in the middle of the night, and as I came to him in his room, he had rolled his iron trundle bed from the farthest end of the room up to the window and was observing the sky. 'Haven't you seen anything in the sky?' he asked me, and when I answered in the negative: 'Then just run to the guard station and ask the sentry whether he hasn't seen anything.' I ran there; but the sentry had seen nothing, which I reported to my master, who still lay as

KATHARINA MOMMSEN

before and watched the sky resolutely. 'Listen,' he said to me then, 'We are experiencing a significant moment; either we are having an earthquake this instant or we will have one.' And then I was obliged to sit down by him on the bed, and he demonstrated to me what signs he gathered that from."

I [Eckermann] asked the good, old man what kind of weather it had been. "It was very cloudy," he said, "and at the same time not a breath of air was stirring; it was very quiet and oppressive."—I asked him if he had really believed what Goethe said right away. "Yes," he said, "I really believed him; for what he predicted was always right. The next day"—he continued—"my master gave an account of his observations at court, during which a woman whispered in her neighbor's ear: 'Listen! Goethe is raving.' But the duke and the other men had faith in Goethe, and it soon turned out, too, that on that same night a part of Messina was destroyed by an earthquake."

(Eckermann, Conversations with Goethe
November 13, 1823)

Who took a more intimate part at Herder's death than Goethe? Goethe learned that a son of Herder had debts of eighty thalers. . . . Out of concern that the debtor might even trouble Herder's last hours, Goethe paid the whole debt out of his own pocket.

(Heinrich Vosz, 1804)

From Poems of the First Weimar Decade

Cowardly thinking
Fearfully shrinking
Womanish quaking
Wailing and shaking
Ends no misfortune
Won't make you free.

All powers opposing
And with the foe closing;
Show no compliance,
Strong in defiance,
Summon the arms of
What gods there may be.

(1777)

All things the Gods are bestowing, the immortal ones,
On their favorites all;
All the pleasures, the immortal ones,
All the sorrows, the immortal ones, all.

Thus I sang recently as, deep in a glorious moonlit night, I climbed out of the river that flows through the meadow by my garden; and that proves daily to be true in my case. I cannot help but recognize *good fortune* as my dearest one, but in return it troubles me, too, like a beloved woman.

(To Countess Auguste zu Stolberg
July 17, 1777)

KATHARINA MOMMSEN

Charlotte von Stein, from a Self-Portrait.

The only one, Lida, whom you are able to love,
You do demand for yourself and with right.
And he is wholly yours.
Since I am far from you,
Seems this swift-paced existence
With its loud commotion
Forms a gentle gauze through which I seem to discern
Evermore as through clouds your figure:
It glows for me friendly and true
As through the changeable rays of the Northern
Lights the eternal stars shine.
   (To Charlotte von Stein from a trip to Gotha on October 9, 1781)

Another

O'er all the hilltops
Is quiet now,
In all the tree tops
Hearest thou
Hardly a breath;
The birds are asleep in the trees:
Wait; soon like these
Thou, too, shalt rest.

Wanderer's Night Song

Thou that from the heavens art,
Every pain and sorrow stillest,
And the doubly wretched heart
Doubly with refreshment fillest,
I am weary with contending!
Why this rapture and unrest?
Peace descending
Come, ah, come into my breast!

Translated by Henry Wadsworth Longfellow
(1776 and 1780)

KATHARINA MOMMSEN

From To the Moon

Happy man, that rancor-free
Shows the world his door;
One companion by—and both
In a glow before

Something never guessed by men
Or rejected quite:
Which, in mazes of the breast,
Wanders in the night.

Translated by J.F. Nims
(1777)

Italian Journey

There was little wanting but that I would really have stayed in Italy.
(Conversation with C.F. von Reinhard, 1807)

Experiences and Changes in Italy

Though I may still be the same, I believe I am changed to the very marrow of my bones . . .
I shall reckon a second birthday, a true rebirth, from the day when I first set foot in Rome . . .
Outside of Rome one has no idea of how one will be schooled here. One must be reborn, so to speak, and one looks back on one's former ideas as on one's baby shoes . . .
The rebirth that has refashioned me from the inside out continues ever to have an effect. I thought I would certainly learn something right here; but I never thought that I would have to go so far back in school. . . . The more I have to renounce myself, the more it pleases me. . . . At the same time as my artistic sense it is my ethical sense that is undergoing a great renovation.
(Rome, December 2 to 20, 1786)

A few hours ago I arrived here, have already glanced around the city, seen the Olympic Theater and the buildings of Palladio. . . . And this I will say about Palladio: He was a very profound and, through and through, a great man. . . . There is really something divine in his designs, quite like the strength of a great poet who creates out of truth and lies a third element whose borrowed existence enchants us. . . .
(Vicenza, September 19, 1786)

KATHARINA MOMMSEN

My titanic ideas were but creatures of the air that gave a premonition of a more serious era. Now I undertake the study of the human figure, which is the *non plus ultra* of all human knowledge and activity. My diligent preparatory training in the study of the whole of nature, especially osteology, helps me to make great strides. Now I am seeing, now I am finally enjoying, the best that is left to us from antiquity, the statues. Yes, I can easily understand that one can study for a lifetime and at the end might still exclaim: *Now* I see, *now* I finally enjoy.

(Rome, January 10, 1787)

I had promised to visit the Duchess of Giovane, who lived in the castle Capo di Monte, where they let me find my own way up many steps, through many corridors, until in a large and lofty room that had no special view I found a handsome young woman with very sensitive and well-bred conversational ability. —Twilight had already descended, and they had not yet brought candles. We walked back and forth in the room, and she, drawing close to the side of a window covered by shutters, pushed open a shutter, and I beheld what one sees only once in a lifetime. If she did it on purpose to surprise me, then she accomplished her purpose. We were standing at a window of the upper story, with Vesuvius directly before us; the lava flowing down, whose flame, since the sun had long set, glowed clearly and began to gild the vapor accompanying it; the mountain roaring violently, over it a huge, stationary cloud of steam, its various masses split in a flash and bodily illuminated at each eruption. From there down to the sea a streak of incandescence and glowing steam; moreover, sea and earth, cliff and underbrush distinct in the twilight, clear and peaceful in an enchanted repose. To take all this in at a glance and to behold, as the realization of the most wondrous picture, the full moon rising from behind the mountain cannot help but inspire amazement.

(Italian Journey II, Naples
June 2, 1787)

Goethe in the Roman Campagna. Oil painting by J.H.W. Tischbein, 1786.

KATHARINA MOMMSEN

Vesuvius in March, 1787. Drawing by Goethe.

KATHARINA MOMMSEN

Scientific Studies in Italy – Concept of the Primordial Plant

I will turn with my narration once more to the sea; today I saw there the households of the sea snails, the patella, and the common crab and took great delight in it. What a precious, magnificent thing each living being is! How fitted to its situation, how true, how being! How much my little bit of study of nature profits me, and how I delight in pursuing it. But since it can be communicated, I do not want to provoke my friends with mere exclamations.

(Venice, October 9, 1786)

The botanical garden is all the more pleasing and cheerful. . . . It is delightful and instructive to walk around among vegetation that is strange to us. Among usual plants, as well as among other objects long since familiar, we eventually think nothing at all, and what is seeing without thinking? Here in this variety newly confronting me, that thought becomes more and more active: That all kinds of plants could perhaps evolve from one. Only in this way would it be possible to actually determine the species and varieties, which, it seems to me, hitherto has been done very arbitrarily. I have come to a standstill at this point in my botanical philosophy, and I do not see how I will extricate myself. The depth and the breadth of this business appear to me absolutely equal.

(Padua, September 27, 1786)

Furthermore, I must confide to you that I am very close to the secret of plant reproduction and organization, and that it is as simple as could possibly be imagined. The finest observations can be made in this location. The main point, where the seed is hidden, I have discovered quite clearly and without a doubt;

everything else I also see in general, and only a few points must still be determined. The archetypal plant proves to be the most singular creation in the world, for which nature itself will envy me. With this model and the key to it one can then invent plants ad infinitum that must be consistent, that is: those that could exist even if they do not exist and that are not just artistic or poetic shadows and illusions but have an intrinsic truth and necessity. The same law can be applied to all other living things.

(Naples, May 17, 1787)

Two years after his return from Italy, Goethe's "Attempt to Explain the Metamorphosis of Plants" appeared. Concerning the significance of Spinoza for Goethe, the most important admission can be found in an insignificant place:

But for the present I want to acknowledge that after Shakespeare and Spinoza the greatest influence on me came from Linnaeus.

(The Story of My Botanical Study, 1817)

KATHARINA MOMMSEN

Concerning His Return to Weimar

I can indeed say: I have found myself again in this year and a half of solitude; but as what? —As artist! Whatever else I am, you will judge and use. During your continuous, active life you have expanded and strengthened more and more that princely recognition of how men can be used; I gladly submit myself to this judgment. Look upon me as a guest, by your side let me fill up the whole measure of my existence and enjoy my life to the full; thus my strength, like a spring, now opened, collected, purified, may easily be directed from the heights, hither or yon, according to your purpose.

(To Duke Carl August, Rome
March 17, 1788)

After Goethe's return from Italy Christiane Vulpius, a worker in a flower factory, became his mistress. He took her and her family members into his household. She created for him a "pleasant relationship of domestic companionship" and bore him five children. In 1806 their common-law marriage was legalized after Christiane's bravery had protected Goethe from plundering soldiers.

Today I am commemorating an epoch of my own, my married state is eight years old and the French Revolution is seven.

(To Schiller, July 13, 1796)

But at the same time a diversion was to alienate me from the world, namely, a most decisive turning toward nature, to which I was driven by my own peculiar inclination in a very individual manner. Here I found neither master nor companions and had to rely on myself. In the solitude of the woods and gardens, in the gloom of my dark room I would have remained completely isolated, had not a happy domestic relationship been able sweetly to refresh me during this strange period. The *Roman Elegies*, the *Venetian Epigrams* fit into this time.

(*Campaign in France*, 1792, "Interruption")

Christiane Vulpius, sketched by Goethe, ca. 1788/89.

                    KATHARINA MOMMSEN

. . . an olive-complexioned girl, whose
Dark and plentiful hair, glistening, covered her brow,
Shorter ringlets curled round a neck that was graceful and slender,
  Wavy, unbraided hair rose from the top of her head.
And I recognized her; as she hurried I held her: and sweetly
  She, most willing to learn, soon paid me back each caress.
Oh, how delighted I was! . . .

(From Roman Elegy IV*)*
Translated by Michael Hamburger

Do not regret, my darling, the promptness of your surrender!
  I think no less of you now, nor did you lose my respect.
Eros has arrows of various kinds: some seem just to scratch us,
  And as the slow venom works, so the heart sickens for years.
But there are others, strong-feathered and freshly pointed and sharpened—
  Right to the marrow they pierce, quickly they kindle the blood.
In the heroic age, when a god fell in love with a goddess,
  Passion was born at a glance, and in a trice was appeased.

(From Roman Elegy III*)*
Translated by David Luke

Happy now I can feel the classical climate inspire me,
  Past and present at last clearly, more vividly speak.
Here I take their advice, perusing the works of the ancients
  With industrious care, pleasure that grows every day.
But throughout the nights by Amor I'm differently busied,
  If only half improved, doubly delighted instead.
Also, am I not learning when at the shape of her bosom
  Graceful lines, I can glance, guide a light hand down her hips?
Only thus I appreciate marble; reflecting, comparing,
  See with an eye that can feel, feel with a hand that can see.
True, the loved one besides may claim a few hours of the daytime,
  But in the night hours as well makes full amends for the loss.
For not always we're kissing; often hold sensible converse.

When she succumbs to sleep, pondering, long I lie still.
Often too in her arms I've lain composing a poem,
    Gently with fingering hand count the hexameter's beat
Out on her back; she breathes, so lovely and calm in her sleeping
    That the glow from her lips deeply transfuses my heart.
Amor meanwhile refuels his lamp and remembers the times when
    Them, his triumvirs of verse, likewise he's served and obliged.

(Roman Elegy V)
Translated by Michael Hamburger

After the death of his mother Goethe puts Christiane in his will:

To wit: I appoint herewith my son August, offspring of myself and Christiane Vulpius, my friend and member of my family for many years, to be my sole heir titulo institutionis honorabili; to his aforementioned mother, on the other hand, I bequeath the benefit of all that which I possess in this country at the time of my death, so that she shall remain during her lifetime in uninterrupted possession of the same and collect the income therefrom without executing a bond of usufruct, still under the condition that she expend in a motherly fashion what is necessary for the education of our son.

KATHARINA MOMMSEN

Verses in Memory of Christiane

June 6, 1816 (the day of the death of Goethe's wife Christiane)

You attempt, O sun, but so vainly
To shine through the clouds where I'm tossed now!
My lifetime's whole profit is plainly
Lament for the one that I've lost now.

———————

I wish I had me a pretty wife
Who wasn't so serious about her life,
But at the same time could understand it:
The best way for me was the way I planned it.

———————

I've kept in my poems I'm sure
God and my little one pure.

———————

Just let me have my memory
To keep as happy legacy.

Direction of the Weimar Court Theater
(1791-1817)

[Goethe:] The main point was that the Grand Duke gave me a completely free hand, and I could direct and do as I wanted. I did not look for magnificent scenery and a splendid wardrobe, but I looked for good plays. From tragedy to farce, every genre was fine with me; but a play had to be something special to find favor. It had to be important and sound, bright and graceful, but above all wholesome and had to have an intrinsic virtue. Everything morbid, weak, lachrymose, and sentimental, as well as everything hideous, horrible, and offensive to good morals was excluded once and for all; I would have been afraid of demoralizing the actors and the public with them.

(To Eckermann, March 22, 1825)

What the Weimar theater accomplished under this direction that was excellent in regard to rhetorical considerations is well known, less known is how this was brought about.

The illustrious poet had to concern himself all the more with training the actors of his theater in delivery, since he had resolved to make his public familiar with the dramatic poetry of all nations, something that he accomplished, too, inasmuch as Sophocles and Aristophanes, Plautus and Terence, Shakespeare, Calderon, Alfieri and Goldoni, Corneille, Racine, Voltaire, and Moliere passed over his stage between the national plays and masterpieces.

The method that Goethe used to produce a dramatic poetical work on the stage was truly that of a musical conductor, and he loved to use music as an example in all the rules that he established and to speak symbolically of it in all his instructions. The delivery was directed by him in the rehearsals just in the

KATHARINA MOMMSEN

way an opera is practiced. The tempos, fortes, and pianos, the crescendo and diminuendo and so forth were determined by him and watched over with the most scrupulous severity; and one should certainly not think that such a proceeding impaired the nature and truth of the reading. It was the firm ground on which the actor could abandon himself with confidence to inspiration and to emotion in his performance, if only, sustained by talent, he was capable of emotion and inspiration.

(P.A. Wolff
On Delivery in the Tragedy, 1827)

Goethe never kept people waiting at rehearsals. . . . How attentively they listened when his voice resounded from the depths of the parterre, surpassing the voice of the most talented actor in strength, depth, and melody. His direction of the theater was, as everything that Goethe undertook, methodical, accordingly his orders were comprehensible and forceful, like a higher law. . . . One day the master remarked sarcastically: "Herr Oels, we have seen enough of your hind part; do show us your face again!" In an instant the abashed performer stood facing his chief. . . . In the rehearsal of Schiller's *Tell* the tenor Moltke was playing the role of the shepherd. At the beginning of the piece the shepherd pushed forward to the middle of the stage as soon as he was to speak, whereby the symmetry of the group was disturbed. Goethe called his attention to it and had the scene repeated. But our tenor lapsed into the same error. Then the master ordered "Stop!", came up on the stage, pointed out Moltke's place to him, placed himself between him and the other persons in the play, took him by the arm, and bade the scene be repeated. Moltke pulled and jerked as soon as he was to speak; but Goethe did not waver or yield and thus put the all too active singer straight. Certainly no guarantee is necessary that this event produced general merriment.

(K. Eberwein
Goethe as Theater Director)

It was at the performance of *Wallenstein's Camp* where, by Goethe's order, for the first time the Mister, Madame, and Mademoiselle in front of the names of the members of the cast were omitted. I asked Goethe about the reason for this arrangement; it was his opinion that the name of an artist was sufficient; there were very many misters and madames in this world but very few artists.

(Memoirs of the Actor Genast
in October, 1798)

[Goethe:] In our theater there was no lack of ladies who were beautiful and young and at the same time of great sweetness of spirit. —I felt myself passionately attracted to some of them; also the possibility existed that they were willing to oblige me. But I composed myself and said: *No farther!* —I knew my position and knew what I owed to it. I stood here not as a private person but as the director of an institution whose success was more important to me than my momentary personal happiness. If I had engaged in any sort of love affair, then I would have been like a compass that cannot possibly show the correct direction when it has next to it a magnet working upon it. However, by keeping myself totally pure and always remaining my own master, I also remained master of the theater, and I never lacked the necessary respect without which all authority is very soon lost.

(To Eckermann, March 22, 1825)

 KATHARINA MOMMSEN

Reluctantly Goethe takes part in a war one single time. In the *Campaign in France* he portrays the defeat that in 1792 brought the twenty-year supremacy of the French Revolutionary Army.

Campaign in France
Bombardment of Valmy.
"Cannon fever" foolhardily tested by Goethe

Earlier we had seen the enemy encamped and deployed before the woody area; it could no less be seen that new troops were arriving; it was Kellermann who then joined with Dumouriez in order to make up his left wing. Our soldiers were consumed with the desire to attack the French; officers as well as ordinary soldiers cherished the fervent wish that the general might attack at this moment; our vigorous advance seemed also to indicate it. But Kellermann had positioned himself too advantageously; and now the bombardment began, about which so much is told, the immediate violence of which, however, cannot be described, not even recalled in the imagination.

The main road lay by this time far behind us; we advanced continually to the west, when suddenly an adjutant came galloping up, who ordered us back; we had been brought too far, and now we received the command to return over the road and, directly on its left flank, to support the right wing. This was done, and so we formed a front opposite the outer defenses of La Lune, which could be seen on the heights about a quarter of an hour in front of us on the road. Our commanding officer came toward us; he had just brought up half a troop of horse artillery; we received orders to advance under its cover and found on the way an old mounted sergeant lying on the field stretched out, the first victim of the day. We rode on quite confidently; we saw the defenses closer; the battery posted there fired busily.

But soon we found ourselves in a strange situation. Cannonballs flew at us wildly, though we could not imagine where they might be coming from; we were, after all, advancing behind an allied battery, and the enemy cannon on the hill opposite was far too distant to have been able to reach us. I stopped sideways opposite the front and had the strangest view: The balls fell by the dozen in front of the troop of cavalry, fortunately not ricocheting, burrowing into the soft ground; but mire and mud bespattered man and horse; the black horses, held together as much as possible by capable riders, snorted and raged; the whole crowd was, without parting or becoming disordered, in surging motion. . . .

Meanwhile, the bombardment still continued. Kellermann had a dangerous position near the mill of Valmy, for which the fire was actually intended. There a powder wagon blew up, and there was rejoicing over the trouble that it might have caused among the enemy. And so everything, whether in the line of fire or not, remained just spectator and listener. We stopped on the road to Chalons by a signpost that pointed to Paris.

This capital city lay behind us, but the French army was between us and our homeland. More extensive obstacles had perhaps never been presented to a highly apprehensive person, who had unceasingly studied an exact map of the war theater for four weeks.

Nevertheless, momentary necessity asserted its rights even in view of the immediate future. Our hussars had fortunately intercepted several breadcarts that were supposed to go from Chalons to the army and was bringing them along to the highway. It had to seem strange to us to be stationed between Paris and Sainte Menehould, so those at Chalons could in no way suspect the enemy army to be on the way to them. For a gratuity the hussars gave up some of the bread; it was the finest white; the Frenchman is terrified of every black crumb. I distributed more than one loaf among those closely associated with me, with the stipulation that they keep a share of it for me for the following days. Also, I found an opportunity for still another piece of foresight: A hunter from the retinue had in like manner made a bargain with these hussars for an excellent wool blanket; I offered him an arrangement whereby he let me have it for three nights, each night for eight groschen, while he should keep it in the daytime. He considered these terms to be very favorable; the blanket had cost him a gulden, and after a short time he got it back again with a profit. But I, too, could be content; my fine woolen covers from Longwy had remained behind with the baggage and now, lacking all accommodation outside of my coat, I had acquired still a second shelter.

KATHARINA MOMMSEN

All of this took place under the continuous accompaniment of the cannons' roar. On this day ten thousand rounds were squandered by each side, in the course of which only twelve hundred men fell on our side and even these were completely unavailing. The heavens became clear because of the frightful concussion, for the cannon were fired just as if it were a platoon firing, unevenly, sometimes diminishing, sometimes increasing. In the afternoon at one o'clock, after some interruption, it was the most violent; the earth shook in a completely real sense, and still there was not the slightest change in the positions. No one knew what would come of it.

I had heard so much about "cannon fever"—nervousness under fire—and wished to know what the real nature of it was. Boredom and an imagination that was attracted to every danger to daring, even to foolhardiness, lured me to ride quite calmly up to the defenses of La Lune. This was occupied by our side again but furnished, nevertheless, a very wild appearance. The roofs riddled with shot, the bundles of wheat scattered about, the mortally wounded stretched out here and there on it, and in between sometimes still a cannonball that, gone astray, clattered in the ruins of the tiled roofs.

All alone, left to my own devices, I rode left on the heights and could clearly survey the favorable position of the French; they were located as if in an amphitheater, surrounded by great calm and security, yet, with Kellermann on the left wing, more easily accessible.

There I encountered good company; they were familiar officers from the general staff and the regiment and were very astonished to find me here. They wanted to take me back with them again; I spoke to them, however, about special objectives, and they abandoned me without further ado to my well-known peculiar caprices.

I had now arrived entirely in that area over which the cannonballs were playing; the sound is strange enough, as if it were composed of the humming of a top, the splashing of water, and the trilling of a bird. They were less dangerous because of the damp ground; wherever one fell, it remained fixed, and so my foolish experimental ride was at least protected against the danger of ricochet.

Under these circumstances I could nevertheless recognize that something unusual was happening within me; I paid particular attention to it, and still the feeling could only be communicated by comparisons. It seemed as if one were in a very hot place and also completely permeated by the same heat, so that one felt completely like the element in which one found oneself. One's eyes lost nothing in regard to strength or clarity; but it was nevertheless as if the world had a certain red-brown tinge that made the situation, as well as the objects, still more intimidating. I could notice nothing concerning the circulation of my blood, but rather it seemed to me much more that everything was swallowed in that glow. From this, it now becomes clear in what sense this condition can be called a fever. Meanwhile it remains noteworthy that this terrible anxiety is conveyed to us only through our ears; for the thunder of the cannon, the howling, whistling, crashing of the balls through the air really is the actual origin of these sensations.

When I had ridden back and was completely safe, I found it noteworthy that all the glow was immediately quenched and not the slightest bit of the feverish agitation remained. Furthermore, this condition belongs to the least desirable of states; and I found, among my esteemed and noble comrades in arms, scarcely one who had expressed a really passionate propensity toward it.

Thus the day had passed away; the French stood immovable, Kellermann had also taken a more comfortable position; our people were pulled out of the fire and it was just as if nothing had happened. The greatest consternation spread over the army. Just that morning they had thought of nothing but impaling the French and eating them up, yes, this unconditional confidence in such an army, in the Duke of Braunschweig, had lured me, too, to take part in this dangerous expedition; but now each one went along by himself, no one looked at anyone else, or if it happened at all, it was to call down an oath or to curse. Just as it was becoming night we had happened to form a circle, in the middle of which we could not even light a fire as usual; most of us were silent; a few were talking, and really each one was lacking in deliberation and judgment. Finally they asked me to tell what I thought about it, for as a rule I had amused and enlivened the assemblage with short sayings; this time I said: "Here and now a new epoch of world history begins, and you can say you were there."

(The night of September 19, [1792])

                                                    KATHARINA MOMMSEN

Wilhelm Meister's Apprenticeship

Mignon, the strange child

Philine invited both of her companions to come with her to her lodgings because, as she said, the public performance could be seen better from her windows than in the other inn.

When they arrived, they found the stage erected and the background decorated with suspended rugs. The springboards were already in place, the slack rope fastened to the post, and the tightrope pulled over the trestles. The plaza was rather full of people and the windows occupied by spectators of sundry kinds.

First Pagliacci warmed up the crowd and put them in a good mood with some silliness that spectators always are given to laugh about. Some children, whose bodies exhibited the most unusual dislocations, aroused sometimes astonishment, sometimes horror; and Wilhelm could not contain his deep sympathy, when he saw the child in whom he had taken an interest at first glance produce the unusual positions with some effort. But soon the merry gymnasts provoked a brisk diversion when, first individually, then one after another, and at last all together, they turned flips forwards and backwards in the air. Loud applause and shouting was heard from the whole assembly.

But then their attention was turned to a completely different affair. The children, one after the other, had to walk the rope and, of course, the novices were first, so that through their exercise they would extend the performance and bring to light the difficulty of the art. Some men and some grown ladies also emerged, who had considerable dexterity, but they were still not Monsieur Narcissus nor still not Mademoiselle Landrinette.

Finally those two also made their appearance out of a type of tent from behind red curtains, which had been spread, and fulfilled with their pleasant forms and elegant adornment the expectations that the spectators had happily cherished till now. He, a blithe youth of middle size, with black eyes and a thick pigtail; she, no less well and strongly built; both made their appearance one after the other on the rope with nimble movements, leaps, and unusual postures. Her agility, his daring, the precision with which both executed their clever feats, heightened the general enjoyment with every step and leap. The pleasing demeanor with which they conducted themselves, the obvious effort of the others around them gave them the appearance of being lord and master of the whole troop, and everyone considered them worthy of the position.

The animation of the crowd spread to the spectators at the windows, the ladies looked resolutely at Narcissus, the gentlemen at Landrinette. The people shouted with enthusiasm and the more refined audience did not refrain from clapping; it reached the point that they scarcely had time to laugh at Pagliacci. Just a few slipped away when some of the troop members, in order to collect money, pressed through the crowd with tin plates.

"They have done their job well, it seems to me," Wilhelm said to Philine, who was next to him at the window, "I admire the way they know how to make even modest little tricks worthwhile, when they are mounted appropriately little by little and at the proper time, and how they cooperate to make a whole out of the ineptitude of their children and the virtuosity of their best performers, that at first aroused our attention and then entertained us in the most pleasant way."

The people had gradually dispersed, and the plaza had become empty, while Philine and Laertes got into an argument about the appearance and skill of Narcissus and Landrinette and were teasing each other in turn. Wilhelm saw the strange child standing on the street with other playing children and drew Philine's attention to it, and immediately in her lively way she called and beckoned to the child, and since it was not willing to come, she clattered singing down the stair and brought it back up.

"Here is our mystery," she exclaimed as she drew the child through the doorway. It stayed by the entrance as if it were about to slip out again, put its right hand on its breast, its left on its forehead, and bowed deeply.

"Don't be afraid, dear little one," said Wilhelm, as he started toward her. She looked at him with uncertain eyes and went a few steps nearer.

"What is your name?" he asked.

"They call me Mignon."

"How old are you?"

"No one has counted my years."

"Who was your father?"

"The big devil is dead."

"Now that is strange enough!" Philine cried out. They asked her a few other things; she produced her answers in broken German and in a seriously solemn manner, while each time she placed her hands on her breast and her head and bowed deeply.

Wilhelm couldn't look at her enough. His eyes and his heart were irresistibly attracted to the mysterious plight of this creature. He judged she must be twelve to thirteen years old; her body was well-shaped, though her limbs showed either the promise of future growth or else of having been retarded. Her features were not regular but striking; her brow mysterious, her nose extraordinarily beautiful, and her mouth, although it seemed to be too determined for her age and her lips often twitched to one side, was still guileless and charming enough. The rather dark color of her skin was scarcely noticeable through the makeup. Her appearance impressed itself deeply upon Wilhelm; he continued to look at her, was silent, and forgot those present in his contemplation. Philine woke him out of his half-dream by handing the child some leftover candy and indicating to her that she should leave. She made a bow as before and was out of the door like a flash.

(Book 2, Chapter 4)

Philine's wantonness

After a short time that he had spent sitting and staring into space, troubled by various thoughts, Philine came strolling through the door singing and sat down by him, one might really almost say on him, she drew so close to him, leaned on his shoulder, played with his curls, caressed him, and spoke the fairest words in the world to him. She pleaded with him that he should really stay and not leave her alone in the company where she could not help but die of boredom; she could not endure it anymore under one roof with Melina and for that reason had taken lodging over here.

He sought in vain to refuse her, to make her understand that he neither could nor should remain. She did not cease her pleas, even unexpectedly wound her arms around his neck and kissed him with the most energetic expression of desire.

"Are you mad, Philine?" Wilhelm exclaimed, as he tried to disengage himself, "to make a public street witness to these caresses that I do not in any way deserve. Let me go; I cannot and I will not stay."

"And I will hold you fast," she said, "and I will kiss you here on the public street until you promise me what I want. I'll die laughing," she continued, "after these intimacies people will surely take me for your wife of a month, and the married men who see such a charming scene will commend me to their wives as a model of unconstrained, childlike affection."

Some people passed by just then, and she caressed him most charmingly, and he, in order not to create a scandal, was forced to play the role of the patient husband. Then she made faces at the people behind their backs and perpetrated all sorts of impertinencies, until at last he had to promise to stay to-day and tomorrow and day after tomorrow.

"You are a regular clod!" she said then, meanwhile turning him loose, "and I am a fool to waste so much friendliness on you." She stood up out of sorts and went a few steps; then she turned back laughing and exclaimed: "I really believe that is why I am crazy about you, I just want to go get my knitting so I'll have something to do. Stay there, so I can find my stone man on a stone bench again."

This time she was unfair to him; for however much he endeavored to stay away from her, still if at this moment he had found himself with her in a lonesome bower, he would probably not have let her caresses go unreturned.

She went into the house, after she had thrown him a wanton glance. He had no business following her, on the contrary, her behavior had aroused a new aversion in him; but he rose from the bench, without knowing himself just why, to go after her.

(Book 2, Chapter 12)

Philine's unselfishness

"Philine," Wilhelm said, "I owe you many thanks already in connection with the misfortune that happened to us, and I do not want to see my obligation to you increased. I am uneasy as long as you are around me; for I know no way I can repay you for your trouble. Give me my things that you rescued in your trunk, join the rest of the company, look for another lodging, accept my thanks

 KATHARINA MOMMSEN

and the gold watch as a small token of gratitude; only leave me, your presence upsets me more than you believe."

She laughed in his face when he had finished. "You are a fool," she said, "you will never learn. I know better what is good for you; I will stay; I will not stir from this spot. I have never counted on the gratitude of men, so not on yours either; and if I love you, what business is that of yours?"

(Book 4, Chapter 9)

The explanation of Philine's declaration in Goethe's autobiography:

But what particularly attracted me to Spinoza was the infinite unselfishness that was evident in every sentence. That singular expression: "Who loves God must not demand that God return his love," with all the premises on which it rests, with all the consequences that originate in it, filled all my contemplation. To be unselfish in everything, most selfless in love and friendship, was my greatest desire, my axiom, my habitual exercise, so that those later impudent words: "If I love you, what business is it of yours?" were spoken straight from the heart.

(*Truth and Poetry*, Book 14)

Two Songs of Mignon

Knowst thou the land of flowering lemon trees?
In leafage dark the golden orange glows,
From azure sky there wafts a gentle breeze,
Calm the myrtle, high the laurel grows,
Knowst thou it still?
  Aiee, aiee,
There would I go, beloved mine, with thee.

Knowst thou the house? Its column-bedded roof,
The shining hall, the inner room aglow,
The marble statues gaze but do not move:
What have they done, poor child, to hurt thee so?
Knowst thou it still?
  Aiee, aiee,
There would I go, protector mine, with thee.

Knowst thou the mountain, stepping up through cloud?
The mule in mist treads out his path; a cave,
And in it dwells the ancient dragon brood;
The crag swoops down and over it the wave;
Knowst thou it still?
  Aiee, aiee,
There goes the way, father, for thee and me.

Translated by Christopher Middleton

KATHARINA MOMMSEN

None but a lover knows
My lonely yearning,
All sorrow when joy goes,
No more returning,
I search the skies above,
The world around me.
Ah! Far away the love
That once had found me!
My heartsick longing grows,
My inner burning.
None but a lover knows
My lonely yearning.

Translated by Freda Morrill Abrams

Wilhelm in the Hall of the Tower Society

He had no further time to think; for the curtain opened again, and a man stood before his eyes whom he recognized immediately as the country clergyman who had made that boat excursion with him and the merry party; he looked like the Abbe, though he did not seem to be the same person. With a serene face and a dignified expression the man began: "The duty of the teacher of man is not to guard against error but to guide the erring one, even to allow him to quaff his error out of a full cup—that is the wisdom of teachers. Who only gets a taste of his error, keeps house with it for a long time; he delights in it as in infrequent pleasure, but he who drains it all must learn to know it, if he is not mad." The curtain closed again, and Wilhelm had time to contemplate. "What error can the man be speaking of," he said to himself, "except the one that has followed me my whole life, that I sought education where none could be found, that I imagined I could acquire a talent to which I had not the slightest predisposition."

(Book 7, Chapter 9)

Wilhelm's Departure from the Theater

I am leaving the theater and I will associate with men whose intimate acquaintance must lead me in every sense to a pure and certain occupation.

(Book 7, Chapter 8)

Schiller as Goethe's Friend

Moreover, it is some of the best good fortune of my life that I lived to see the completion of this work [Wilhelm Meister], that it occurs within the period of my strength and aspiration, that I can still draw from this pure source; and the fine relationship that exists between us makes it a true religion to me to make your cause herein my own, to educate everything that is reality in me to become the purest mirror of the spirit, which lives in this frame, and thus in a higher sense of the word to deserve the name of your friend. How vividly I have learned on this occasion that excellence is an influence, that it can have an effect on selfish minds only as an influence, that there is no freedom but love in the face of excellence.

(Schiller to Goethe
July 2, 1796)

Just after I had received your first letter, I began to say something to you about it; now your two subsequent letters surprise me in my truly temporal affairs, truly as voices out of another world to which I can only give ear. Continue to refresh me and encourage me! Through your reflections you enable me to finish the eighth book as soon as I set about it again. I already have information for almost all of your *desideria*, through which, even in my own mind, the whole becomes more united on these points, too, becomes truer and more pleasing. You should by no means become weary of telling me your opinion and keep the book with you this week. What you need about Cellini I will expedite meanwhile, I am writing you only in summary what I still have in mind to do on the eighth book, and then the last draft should be out of our hands by the beginning of August.

Your letters are now my only support, and you must certainly feel how grateful I am to you that you are helping me so suddenly over so many things. Farewell and greetings to your charming wife.

(Goethe to Schiller
July 5, 1796)

KATHARINA MOMMSEN

Faust

The First Part of the Tragedy

As a philanthropist Faust is venerated by the people almost like a saint.

OLD PEASANT:
    Professor, it is good of you
    to deign to be with us today
    and, learned doctor though you are,
    to mingle with us ordinary folk.
    And so accept our finest tankard,
    which we have filled afresh for you;
    I pledge it to you, and I voice the wish
    that it not only slake your thirst,
    but also that each drop it holds
    be one more day that's added to your life.

FAUST:
    Your tankard I accept and its refreshment
    with thanks and wishes of good health to all.

                (THE VILLAGERS *form a circle about* FAUST *and* WAGNER.)

OLD PEASANT:
    It is indeed appropriate
    that on this festive day you come among us;
    as well we know, when times were bad
    you always were disposed to help us!
    Many a man is here alive
    who, at the time your father stopped the plague,
    was snatched by him at the last moment
    from the burning frenzy of his fever.
    You too—you were a young man then—
    would enter every stricken house
    and yet, although they carried off so many corpses,
    you always would come out unharmed,

surviving every trial and test—
by the Helper above our helper was helped.

THE VILLAGERS:
Good health to one who's tried and true,
and may he be our help for many years to come!

FAUST:
Offer your homage to the Helper above
Who teaches that we all should help each other.

(FAUST and WAGNER continue their walk.)

WAGNER:
What feelings, sir, you must derive
from the respect of all these people for your greatness!
How happy is the man who is allowed
to turn his talents to such good account!
Some father points you out to his young boy,
and people ask your name, stand still and crowd about you,
the fiddle stops, the dancers pause.
As you move on, they stand in rows
and fling their caps into the air—
a little more, and they would genuflect
as if the blessed sacrament were going by!

(v. 981-1021)
Translated by Stuart Atkins

The exorcism of the poodle. Mephistopheles appears.

FAUST:
. . .
Being damned and reprobate,
can you read this token?—
Him that never was create,
Him whose name must not be spoken,
Who pervades the universe,
though transpierced by lance accursed.
Driven back of the stove by the spell,

KATHARINA MOMMSEN

it is dilating to elephant size;
filling every bit of space,
it's now about to melt away as mist.
    Stop ascending to the ceiling!
Lie down at your master's feet!
Now you know I make no empty threats.
I can scorch you with sacred fire!
Do not wait until you see
the glowing light of the Trinity,
do not wait until you see
the mightiest of all my arts!

MEPHISTOPHELES (*emerging from behind the stove as the mist subsides, dressed as a Goliard*):
   What's all the noise? Sir, how can I be of service?

FAUST:
   So that is what was hidden in the poodle:
   a wandering scholar! The *casus* is amusing.

MEPHISTOPHELES:
   My compliments to your learning, sir!
   you made me sweat profusely.

FAUST:
   What is your name?

MEPHISTOPHELES:
   That seems a pretty question
   from one who is so scornful of the Word
   and who, aloof from mere appearance,
   only aspires to plumb the depths of essence.

FAUST:
   The essence of such as you, good sir,
   can usually be inferred from names
   that, like Lord of Flies, Destroyer, Liar,
   reveal it all too plainly.
   But still I ask, who are you?

MEPHISTOPHELES:
   A part of that force

which, always willing evil, always produces good.

FAUST:

That is a riddle. What does it mean?

MEPHISTOPHELES:

I am the Spirit of Eternal Negation,
and rightly so, since all that gains existence
is only fit to be destroyed; that's why
it would be best if nothing ever got created.
Accordingly, my essence is
what you call sin, destruction,
or—to speak plainly—Evil.

FAUST:

You call yourself a part, yet stand before me whole?

MEPHISTOPHELES:

I only speak the sober truth.
You mortals, microcosmic fools,
may like to think of yourselves as complete,
I am a part of the Part that first was all,
part of the Darkness that gave birth to Light—
proud Light, that now contests the senior rank
of Mother Night, disputes her rights to space;
yet it does not succeed, however much it strives,
because it can't escape material fetters.
Light emanates from matter, lends it beauty,
but matter checks the course of light,
and so I hope it won't be long
before they both have been annihilated.

FAUST:

Now I see your meritorious function:
You can't achieve wholesale destruction
and so you've started out at retail.

MEPHISTOPHELES:

And to be candid, the business doesn't thrive.
This awkward world, this Something

which confronts as foe my Nothing—
despite all I so far have undertaken,
I've failed to get the better of it:
in spite of tempest, earthquake, wave, and fire,
ocean and land are unperturbed!
And as for that stupid stuff, the spawn of beast and man,
there's no way to make inroads on it.
To think how many I've already buried,
yet fresh young blood still keeps on circulating.
On and on—it could make anyone see red!
From air, from water, and from earth
a myriad of germs crawl forth
in dryness, moisture, heat, or cold!
If I had not kept fire for myself,
there would be nothing I could call my own.

FAUST:
And so you raise your frigid fist,
clenched in futile diabolic malice,
against the power of ever-stirring,
beneficent creativity!
You would do well, strange son of Chaos,
to try some other enterprise.

(v. 1304-1384)
Translated by Stuart Atkins

Wager with Mephistopheles

MEPHISTOPHELES:

. . .

Be done with toying with your sorrows
that, vulture-like, consume your being;
the worst society there is could show you
that you are just another human being.
Not that I mean you should be thrust

among the rabble!
I'm not one of the great myself;
but should you wish
to make your way through life with me,
I'll gladly place myself at your disposal
here and now.
I will be your companion
and, if I suit you,
become your servant and your slave!

FAUST:
And in return for this, what am I to do?

MEPHISTOPHELES:
You've lots of time until that needs to be considered.

FAUST:
Oh no! The devil is an egoist
and is not apt, for love of God,
to offer anyone assistance.
State in clear terms what you expect—
there's trouble in the household otherwise.

MEPHISTOPHELES:
I'll bind myself to serve you *here*,
be at your beck and call without respite;
and if or when we meet again *beyond*,
then you will do the same for me.

FAUST:
With the Beyond I cannot be much bothered;
Once you annihilate this world,
the other can have its turn at existing.
This earth's the source of all my joys,
and this sun shines upon my sorrows;
if ever I can be divorced from them,
I do not want to hear still more discussion
of whether there'll be future loves and hates,

                                          KATHARINA MOMMSEN

and whether also, in those spheres,
there's an Above or a Below.

MEPHISTOPHELES:
You can, on these conditions, take the risk.
Commit yourself, and you'll soon have the pleasure
of seeing here what my skills are;
I'll give you things no mortal's ever seen.

FAUST:
And what have you to give, poor devil!
Has any human spirit and its aspirations
ever been understood by such as you?
Of course you've food that cannot satisfy,
red, restless gold that, like quicksilver,
will liquefy when held within your hand,
games at which none can ever win,
a girl who, even in my arms, will with her eyes
pledge her affections to another,
the godlike satisfaction of great honor
that like a meteor is gone at once.
Show me the fruit that, still unplucked, will rot
and trees that leaf each day anew!

MEPHISTOPHELES:
These commissions don't dismay me,
I can oblige you with such marvels.
But, friend, there also comes a time when we prefer
to savor something good in peace and quiet.

FAUST:
If on a bed of sloth I ever lie contented,
may I be done for then and there!
If ever you, with lies and flattery,
can lull me into self-complacency
or dupe me with your sybaritic pleasures,
may that day be the last for me!
This is my wager!

MEPHISTOPHELES:
  Here's my hand!

FAUST:
                    And mine again!
  If I should ever say to any moment:
     Tarry, remain!—you are so fair!
  then you may lay your fetters on me,
  then I will gladly be destroyed!
  Then they can toll the passing bell,
  your obligations then be ended–
  the clock may stop, its hand may fall,
  and time at last for me be ended!

MEPHISTOPHELES:
  Consider well your words–we'll not forget them.

(v. 1635-1707)
Translated by Stuart Atkins

KATHARINA MOMMSEN

Scenes from the Gretchen tragedy

A Street
(FAUST, MARGARETE, *walking past.*)

FAUST:
My lovely young lady, may I perhaps venture
to give you my arm and be your escort?

MARGARETE:
I'm not a young lady, or lovely either,
and need no escort to get home.

(Freeing her arm, exit.)

FAUST:
By God, that girl is a real beauty!
I've never seen one quite like her.
She is all modesty and virtue,
yet there's a bit of pertness too.
As long as I live I won't forget
those glowing cheeks and ruby lips!
Even the way she lowered her eyes
is stamped forever on my heart;
as for the brusqueness of her manner,
that was especially delightful!

(Enter MEPHISTOPHELES.)

You must get me that girl, I tell you.

MEPHISTOPHELES:
Which one?

FAUST:
The one that just went by.

MEPHISTOPHELES:
What, her? She is returning from confession;
the priest absolved her of all sin—
I crept up close to the confessional.
She is an innocent, and so much so
that she had nothing to confess;
over that girl I have no power.

FAUST:
  She's over fourteen, isn't she!

MEPHISTOPHELES:
  You're talking like Jack Reprobate;
  he covets every pretty flower,
  and fancies there's no honest favor
  which can't be plucked if he but tries;
  that isn't always so, however.

FAUST:
  My dear Professor Dogmatist,
  you may spare me your moral lessons!
  And let me tell you very bluntly,
  unless that sweet young thing is lying
  within my arms this very night,
  at stroke of twelve we part forever.

(v. 2605-2638)
Translated by Stuart Atkins

Garden

(MARGARETE *on* FAUST's *arm*; MARTHA *and* MEPHISTOPHELES *walking back and forth.*)

MARGARETE:
  I'm well aware that the gentleman's just being kind
  and condescending so that I won't feel embarrassed.
  You travelers are so accustomed
  to taking anything you get politely.
  I know only too well that my poor conversation
  can't entertain someone with your experience.

FAUST:
  One look or word from you is far more entertaining
  than all the wisdom of this world. (*Kissing her hand.*)

MARGARETE:
  Oh, don't! You really shouldn't! How can you bear to kiss it?
  My hand's so ugly, it's so rough.

                                         KATHARINA MOMMSEN

It's all the work I've had to do—
my mother's so particular. *(Passing from view, with Faust.)*

(v. 3073-3084)

MARGARETE:
Though you but think of me for one short moment,
I shall have ample time to think of you.

FAUST:
You must be much alone?

MARGARETE:
Oh, yes, our household is a modest one,
but still it has to be attended to.
We have no maid; it's up to me to cook and sweep,
to knit and sew, and to be always on my feet;
and Mother is so fussy!
It's not that she needs be so economical;
more than a lot of people, we could be living well—
my father left a nice estate,
a small house, and outside the town, a garden-plot.
But now my days are mostly quiet;
my brother is a soldier,
my little sister's dead.
She was a lot of trouble, to be sure,
but I'd be glad to have it all again,
I loved the child so much.

FAUST:
An angel, if like you!

MARGARETE:
I had the care of her, she loved me very much.
When she was born, my father had already died.

(v. 3106-3126)

FAUST:
  My little angel recognized me right away
  when I was entering the garden?

MARGARETE:
  Didn't you see how I lowered my eyes?

FAUST:
  And you forgive my liberty the other day—
  it really was presumptuous impudence—
  when you were coming out of the cathedral?

MARGARETE:
  I was dismayed, I'd never had that happen;
  till then, nobody could speak ill of me.
  Dear me, I thought, can he have seen in your behavior
  something immodest or improper?
  It was as if he felt he had the right
  to treat me as an ordinary girl.
  Yet to be honest, right away inside me
  something began to intercede for you;
  but just the same I was quite angry with myself
  because I couldn't be still angrier with you.

FAUST:
  Sweet love!

MARGARETE:
                Let me do this!

                              (Picking a daisy, she plucks its petals one by one.)

FAUST:
                              Is it for a bouquet?

MARGARETE:
  No, just a game.

FAUST:
                    How's that?

MARGARETE:
                              Stay there! You'd only laugh.
                                    (Pulling off petals, and murmuring.)

                                        KATHARINA MOMMSEN

FAUST:
  What are you murmuring?

MARGARETE (half aloud):

                    He loves me—loves me not.

FAUST:
  That lovely, that angelic face!

MARGARETE (continuing):
  Loves me—not—loves me—not—

                              (Plucking the last petal, and with elation.)

  He loves me!

FAUST:

              Yes, my child! Let what this flower says
  serve you as oracle. He loves you.
  Do you know what that means? He loves you!

                                          (Clasping her hands.)

MARGARETE:
  I'm trembling!

FAUST:

  Don't be afraid! Look in my eyes,
  let them and let these hands that now clasp yours
  express what tongue can never say:
  complete devotion and a sense of bliss
  that must endure eternally!
  Eternally!—It's end would be despair.
  No end! Never! No end, ever!

(MARGARETE presses his hands, frees herself, and runs off.
                    FAUST stands pensive for a moment, then follows her.)
                                          (v. 3163-3194)
                              Translated by Stuart Atkins

                                                              Prison

FAUST (with keys and a lamp, standing before a small iron door):
  A long-forgotten sense of horror makes me tremble,
  all mankind's miseries have hold of me.

She is lodged here, behind the darkness of this wall,
and faith in human goodness was her crime!
You hesitate to enter where she is,
you are afraid to see her once again!
Go now! Your hesitation but lets death come ever nearer.

(As FAUST *takes hold of the lock, singing is heard from behind the door.)*

[MARGARETE:]
It was mother, the whore!
who put me to death,
and father, poor knave!
the one who did eat me.
The bones that remained,
little sister then laid
in a cool, quiet place;
I changed into a little bird
and fly away in the forest!

FAUST *(unlocking the door):*
She's unaware her lover's listening,
can hear the clanking chains, the rustling straw.

(He enters the cell.)

MARGARETE *(cowering on her pallet):*
O woe! They've come! Death is so bitter!

FAUST *(softly):*
Be quiet! Hush! I've come to set you free.

MARGARETE *(rolling over toward him):*
If you are human, pity me in my distress!

FAUST:
Your cries will wake the sleeping guards!

(He takes hold of her fetters to unlock them).

MARGARETE *(on her knees):*
Headsman, who's given you the right
to treat me thus?
It's only midnight, and you've come to take me.
Have mercy on me, let me live!

                                                KATHARINA MOMMSEN

Is not tomorrow morning soon enough?   (*She rises.*)
I'm still so young, so young,
and yet I am to die already!
I once was pretty, that was my undoing.
I had a lover, now he's far away,
they've torn my bridal wreath, its flowers all lie scattered.
Do not take hold of me so brutally!
Spare me! What harm have I done you?
Don't let me plead in vain,
you know I've never seen you in my life!

FAUST:
Can I get through this misery?

MARGARETE:
I am completely at your mercy now.
First let me just nurse my child again.
All night I have been holding it close to my heart;
to hurt my feelings, they took it from me,
and now they're saying that I killed it.
And I can't ever be happy again.
People are making me their song! It's mean of them!
There's an old story that ends like that,
who gave them the right to say it's mine?

FAUST (*falling at her feet*):
Here at your feet is someone who loves you,
who's come to deliver you from your misery.

MARGARETE (*throwing herself down beside him*):
O let us kneel and ask the saints to aid us!
Look, beneath these stones,
under this sill,
hellfire is seething.
In terrible anger
hear Satan himself
raising an uproar!

FAUST (*loudly*):
  Gretchen! Gretchen!

MARGARETE (*becoming attentive*):
  That was my lover's voice.

(She springs to her feet; the fetters drop to the floor.)

  Where is he? I heard him calling.
  I am free! No one can stop me.
  I want to rush and throw my arms about his neck,
  I want to lie upon his breast!
  There at the door he called out: Gretchen!
  In the howling and clatter of hell,
  and the angry jeering of devils,
  I could tell the sound of that dear, sweet voice.

FAUST:
  I'm here!

MARGARETE:
      It's you! O say so once again!   (*Embracing him.*)
  It's he, it's he! Where are my torments now—
  the fearful prison and the dreadful chains?
  It's you! You've come to rescue me,
  and I am saved!—
  There is the street again
  where I first saw you,
  the happy garden where,
  with Martha, I'm awaiting you.

FAUST (*urging her toward the door*):
  Come! Come along!

MARGARETE:
      Don't hurry! Stay!
  I so much like to be where you are staying.   (*Caressing him.*)

FAUST:
  Make haste!
  Unless you hurry,
  there'll be a dreadful price to pay.

                    KATHARINA MOMMSEN

MARGARETE:

Are you no longer able to return a kiss?
So short a time away from me, my love,
and you've forgotten how to kiss?
Why do I feel so frightened in your arms,
when once your words, your eyes,
brought all of heaven down about me,
and you seemed to want to stifle me with kisses.
Give me a kiss,
or I'll kiss you!   *(Embracing him.)*
Your lips are terribly cold,
they do not speak.
What has become
of the love you had?
Who's stolen it from me!   *(Turning away.)*

FAUST:

Come, follow me! Dear love, have courage!
If you but follow me, I'll hold you to my heart
with all the warmth it has! I beg you only, come!

MARGARETE (turning toward FAUST):

And is it you? And is it really you?

FAUST:

Yes! Come with me!

MARGARETE:

You have undone my chains,
are taking me again into your arms.
But why do you not shrink from me in fear?
Do you, my love, know whom you're setting free?

FAUST:

Come, hurry! Darkness is already waning!

MARGARETE:

I am the one who killed my mother,
I am the one who drowned my child.
Wasn't the baby given to us both,

to you as well? —I hardly can believe it's you!
Give me your hand. Yes, this is not a dream!
Your dear, dear hand! But oh, it's wet.
Wipe it off! I can't help thinking
there's blood on it.
Oh God, what have you done!
Put up your sword,
I beg you.

FAUST:
Let what is past, be past,
or you will be the death of me.

MARGARETE:
No, you must go on living!
I want to tell how the graves should be;
you must see to them tomorrow
the very first thing:
the best place for mother;
my brother close beside;
with me a bit off to the side,
yet not too far away;
and the little one at my right breast.
No one else is to be beside me!—
How lovely it was and what sweet happiness
to nestle up against you!
But I can't do so any more—
it is as if I had to force myself upon you
and you were pushing me away from you.
And still it's you, looking so kind, so good.

FAUST:
Come, if you feel sure of whom I am!

MARGARETE:
Out through there?

FAUST:
To freedom.

KATHARINA MOMMSEN

MARGARETE:
  If the grave's out there
  and death lying in wait, yes!
  From here to my bed of eternal rest,
  and not one step beyond—
  Are you now leaving? Heinrich, would that I could too!

FAUST:
  You can if you but wish! The door is open.

MARGARETE:
  I cannot leave; for me there is no hope.
  Why run away when they are watching for me?
  It's terrible to be reduced to begging,
  and then with a bad conscience too!
  It's terrible to go not knowing where—
  and they will catch me anyhow.

FAUST:
  I'll be with you.

MARGARETE:
  Hurry! Hurry!
  save your poor child!
  Quick! Keep to the path
  that goes up along the brook,
  then over the bridge
  and into the woods
  to the left, by the fence—
  in the pond!
  Grab hold, don't wait!
  See the effort to rise,
  the stirring of life—
  save it, save it!

FAUST:
  Be sensible, I beg you!
  One step, just one! and you'll be free.

MARGARETE:

    If only we were past the hill!

On a rock there, my mother is sitting—

I feel a cold hand grab my hair!

There on a rock my mother is sitting

and feebly shaking her head;

she doesn't wave or nod, her head's too heavy;

she slept too long to ever waken again.

She slept to let us have our happiness.

And those were happy times!

FAUST:

    If pleas and reasons are of no avail,

I'll carry you away against your will.

MARGARETE:

    Let go of me! I won't be forced.

Take your wicked hands off me!

You know that up to now I've done what you have wanted.

FAUST:

    The day dawns gray!—O dearest one!

MARGARETE:

    Day! Yes, the day begins—the day of judgment

that should have been my wedding day!

Let no one know you've been in Gretchen's room.

Alas, no wreath—

what's done can't be undone!

We'll meet again,

but not at a wedding dance.

The crowd is gathering in silence;

the square and streets

won't hold them all.

Hear the knell calling, see the white rod break!

How roughly they tie and handle me,

how quickly they carry me to the block!

The edge that rushes down at me

is darting now toward every neck.

KATHARINA MOMMSEN

All is silence—the silence of the grave!

FAUST:
O, that I never had been born!

MEPHISTOPHELES *(appearing outside the cell)*:
Come! Away, or both of you are lost!
Futile faintheartedness! Delaying and prattling!
My horses are trembling—
there's a first glimmer of dawn.

MARGARETE:
What's that, rising up from below?
That man! Send him away!
Why is he here, in this holy place?
He's come for me!

FAUST:
You shall not die!

MARGARETE:
Divine justice, in you I placed my trust!

MEPHISTOPHELES *(to FAUST)*:
Come, or I'll abandon both of you.

MARGARETE:
I am your child, Father—save me!
Angels and heavenly hosts,
compass me about and keep me safe!
Heinrich! I fear and loathe you.

MEPHISTOPHELES:
She is judged!

VOICE *(from above)*:
She is saved!

MEPHISTOPHELES *(to FAUST)*:
Away, with me!

(He disappears with Faust.)

VOICE *(from within, growing faint)*:
Heinrich! Heinrich!

(v. 4405-4612)
Translated by Stuart Atkins

Faust

The Second Part of the Tragedy

Faust's death. In philanthropical wishful thinking Faust enjoys the highest moment and thereby loses the wager with Mephistopheles.

FAUST:
> A marsh stretching along those mountains
> contaminates what's been reclaimed so far;
> to drain that stagnant pool as well
> would be a crowning last achievement.
> If I can furnish space for many millions
> to live—not safe, I know, but free to work
> in green and fertile fields, with man and beast
> soon happy on the new-made soil
> and settled in beside the mighty hill
> a dauntless people's effort has erected,
> creating here inside a land of Eden—
> then there, without, the tide may bluster to its brim,
> but where it gnaws, attempting to rush in by force,
> communal effort will be quick to close the breach.
> To this idea I am committed wholly,
> it is the ultimate corollary of wisdom:
> he, only, merits freedom and existence
> who wins them every day anew.
> And so, beset by danger, here childhood's years,
> maturity, and age will all be vigorous.
> If only I might see that people's teeming life,
> share their autonomy on unencumbered soil;
> then, to the moment, I could say:
> tarry a while, you are so fair—
> the traces of my days on earth
> will survive into eternity!—

KATHARINA MOMMSEN

Envisioning those heights of happiness,
I now enjoy my highest moment.

> (FAUST *falls backward and is caught by the* LEMURES, *who lay him on the ground.*)

MEPHISTOPHELES:

No pleasure sates him, no success satisfies,
and so he still keeps chasing shapes that always change;
this final, mediocre, empty moment—
the poor wretch wants to cling to it.
He who resisted me with such great vigor
—time triumphs—lies here on the sand an old, old man.
The clock stands still—

LEMURES:

Stands still? As deathly still as midnight!

Now its hand falls.

MEPHISTOPHELES:

It falls, and all is finished.

> (v. 11,554-11,593)
> *Translated by Stuart Atkins*

Mephistopheles does not win Faust's soul. Angels intervene to save him.

MEPHISTOPHELES:

. . .

> (To the FAT DEVILS, *who have short, straight horns.*)

You there, pot-bellied rascals with the fiery cheeks,
fattened on brimstone, your faces fairly shining.
You bullnecked scoundrels with unturning heads!
watch out below for any phosphorescent glow:
that will be Psyche with her wings—his petty soul—
but if you pluck them off, she is a loathsome worm!
The moment I have set my mark upon her,
away with her in flaming cyclone!
 It is your duty, fat-paunched rogues,
to pay attention to the lower regions,

although it is somewhat uncertain
if that is where she would prefer to dwell.
The navel is one place she likes to stay,
so be on guard, or she may slip out there.

You giant clowns, file-leaders everyone,
keep sawing the air—no letting up!—
with arms full length and sharp claws out
to grab the fluttering fugitive.
Her spirit's surely wretched in her present house,
will want to move up right away to something better.

HEAVENLY HOST:
    Heavenly messengers,
    kin to the blest above,
    come, flying, calmly,
    to bring sinners forgiveness
    and new life to dust;
    provide, as you soar
    in leisurely flight,
    all living creatures
    with tokens of love!

(v. 11,656-11,684)

THE ANGELS:
    Fires of holiness!
    Whom they encompass,
    will live in blessed oneness
    with all who are good.
    Let us, together,
    ascend and give praise!
    The air is now purified,
    his spirit may breathe!

(v. 11,817-11,824)

Translated by Stuart Atkins

KATHARINA MOMMSEN

The outcome of the Gretchen tragedy is decided by the Mater Gloriosa.

ANGELS (*hovering in the higher atmosphere, bearing* FAUST's *immortal soul*):
  This worthy member of the spirit world
  is rescued from the devil:
  for him whose striving never ceases
  we can provide redemption;
  and if a higher love as well
  has shown an interest in him,
  the hosts of heaven come
  and greet him with cordial welcome.

(v. 11,934-11,941)

A PENITENT, *alias* GRETCHEN (*clinging to the* MATER GLORIOSA):
  Deign, o deign,
  you who are peerless,
  you who are radiant,
  to look down on my joy—
  the love of my youth,
  no longer unhappy,
  has now returned!

BLESSED BOYS (*circling closer*):
  Already he has grown
  bigger than we,
  and will reward our loving care
  with love still greater:
  as children we were separated
  from all of life's spheres;
  but this man has gained learning,
  he'll be our teacher.

THE PENITENT (GRETCHEN):
  Amid this host of lofty spirits
  our novice hardly knows he's Faust,
  but when he's sensed that here there is new life,
  he quickly will become their peer.

WHO IS GOETHE?

See him work loose from all the bonds
that once enveloped him on earth!
See how his early, youthful vigor
shows to advantage in etherial raiment!
Grant me permission to instruct him—
he still is dazzled by the strange new light.

MATER GLORIOSA:
Come, rise to higher spheres—
Sensing your presence, he will follow!

DOCTOR MARIANUS (*prostrate, in adoration*):
Look up to salvation's eyes,
tender penitents,
so that you may gratefully
be reborn for heaven!—
May all nobler spirits be
eager for thy service;
Virgin, Mother, Queen, and Goddess,
keep us in your grace!

CHORUS MYSTICUS:
All that is transitory
is only a symbol;
what seems unachievable
here is seen done;
what's indescribable
here becomes fact;
Woman, eternally,
shows us the way.

(v. 12,069-12,111)
Translated by Stuart Atkins

KATHARINA MOMMSEN

The Elective Affinities

It seems that the author was motivated to use this strange title because of his continued work in the physical sciences. He may have noticed that in the science of physics very often an ethical comparison is used in order to make something clearer that is far removed from the sphere of human knowledge, and so he has probably also been inclined in an ethical instance to trace a figurative expression having to do with chemistry back to its spiritual origins, all the more so since there is everywhere, after all, only *one* nature and also throughout the realm of serene rational freedom there penetrate incessantly the traces of cheerless, intense necessity that can be obliterated only by a higher hand and perhaps not even in this life.

(Announcement by Goethe, 1809)

The Conflict

The next morning the captain had vanished, and a grateful and sensitive note to his friends was left behind. He and Charlotte had already taken a halfway, monosyllabic leave of each other on the evening before. She perceived it to be a permanent separation and . . . renounced him absolutely and utterly.

In return she believed she could now expect from others the same restraint that she had exerted over herself. It had not been impossible for her; the same should be possible for others. It was with this feeling that she began the conversation with her husband, all the more outspoken and confident, since she perceived that the matter must be settled once and for all.

"Our friend has left us," she said; "now here we are again, sitting across from each other as before, and the important thing for us now should be whether we want to return entirely to the old state of affairs again. . . . Also we have only to choose now to put Ottilie into another situation. . . . She can return to the boarding school . . . or she can be placed with a good family to enjoy all the advantages of an appropriate education with an only daughter."

"Meanwhile," Eduard replied, fairly composed, "Ottilie has become so spoiled by our friendly company that another might hardly be welcome to her."

"We have all become so spoiled," said Charlotte, "and you not the least. Meanwhile, it is a period that compels us to reflection, that admonishes us in earnest to think of what is best for all the members of our small circle and also not to refuse any self-sacrifice."

"At least I do not find it fair," Eduard answered, "that Ottilie should be the victim and that will happen, if she is thrust out now among strange people. The Captain's happy destiny searched him out here; we can allow him to take his leave from us in peace, even with pleasure. Who knows what is in store for Ottilie; why should we be in such a hurry?"

"What is in store for us is rather clear," Charlotte replied with some agitation; and since it was her intention to speak her mind once and for all, she continued: "You love Ottilie, you have grown accustomed to her. Inclination and desire are rising and being nurtured on her part, too. Why should we not articulate in words what every hour acknowledges and confesses to us? Should we not have enough prudence to ask ourselves what will come of it?"

"And if it is not possible to answer that immediately," replied Eduard, who was attempting to control himself, "still so much can be said, that we should first just determine to await what the future will teach us, when we cannot say exactly what will come of something."

"To foresee that here," Charlotte replied, "does not require great wisdom, and this much can be said in any case, that we both are not young enough any more to go blindly along where it is not desirable or proper to go. No one can take care of us anymore; we must be our own friends, our own caretakers. No one expects us to go astray in some outrageous way, no one expects to find us acting in a blameworthy or even ridiculous way."

"Can you find fault with me," replied Eduard, who was incapable of reciprocating the clear and candid speech of his wife, "can you reproach me, if I have Ottilie's happiness at heart? And not just a future one that cannot always be reckoned with, but a present one? Just imagine, honestly and without self-deception, Ottilie snatched from our company and handed over to strange people—I, at all events, do not believe I am inhuman enough to expect such a change of her."

 KATHARINA MOMMSEN

Charlotte became quite aware of the determination of her husband behind his dissimulation. Now for the first time she was conscious of how far he had withdrawn from her. With some emotion she exclaimed: "Can Ottilie be happy if she alienates us! If she tears my husband away from me, a father from his children!"

"Our children, I should think, have been taken care of," Eduard said, smiling and cool; but he added in a somewhat friendlier fashion: "And who is going to think the worst of us right away!"

"The worst lies very close to the passions," Charlotte observed. "Do not reject my good advice as long as there is still time, nor the assistance that I am offering us. In troubled situations that one must act and help who sees the clearest. This time I am that one. Dear, dearest Eduard, leave it to me! Can you expect me so unceremoniously to renounce my well-earned happiness, my finest right, to renounce you?"

"Who said anything about that?" Eduard replied with some embarrassment.

"You did," replied Charlotte, "in that you want to keep Ottilie close by, are you not admitting everything that must come from this? I do not want to press you; but if you cannot prevail over yourself, you will at least not be able to deceive yourself for much longer."

Eduard felt how right she was. The spoken word is frightful when it suddenly expresses that which the heart has long confirmed; and only to elude it for just a moment, Eduard replied: "It is not really clear to me what you have in mind."

"My intention was," Charlotte replied, "to consult with you about the two suggestions. Each one has much good in it. The boarding school would be most appropriate for Ottilie, when I consider what the child is like now. But the greater and more extensive arrangement is more promising, when I consider what she should become. . . ."

Eduard appeared to agree with her, but only in order to look for some reprieve. Charlotte, whose object was to do something decisive, immediately seized the opportunity, since Eduard did not directly oppose it, to set Ottilie's departure, for which she had already prepared everything quietly, for the next day.

Eduard shuddered; he considered himself to be betrayed, and the affectionate speech of his wife to be contrived, artificial, and planned in order to part him from his happiness forever. He seemed to leave the whole thing to her; but inwardly his resolve was formed. In order to get a breathing space, in order to avert the imminent, inconceivable calamity of Ottilie's removal, he decided to abandon his house, but not completely without the previous knowledge of Charlotte, whom he nevertheless knew how to deceive with the excuse that he did not want to be present at Ottilie's departure, even that he did not want to see her again from this moment on. Charlotte, who believed she had won, gave him all assistance. He ordered his horses, gave his valet the necessary instructions about what he should pack and how he should follow him, and so, as he was about to leave, he sat down and wrote.

EDUARD TO CHARLOTTE

The evil, my dear, that has befallen us may be curable or not, but this I feel, if I am not to despair in this moment, then I must find a respite for myself, for us all. By sacrificing myself I can make a demand. I am leaving my house and will return only under more favorable, calmer expectations. You are meanwhile to occupy it, but with Ottilie. I want to know that she is with you, not among strangers. Look after her, treat her as usual, as formerly, but really even more lovingly, with more friendliness, and more sensitivity. I promise not to seek out a secret relationship with Ottilie. Leave me rather for a time completely ignorant of how you are living; I intend to think the best. You should think the same of me. Only this will I ask you, most sincerely, most fervently: Make no attempt to put Ottilie anywhere else, to place her in a new situation. Beyond the range of your castle, your park, entrusted to strangers, she belongs to me, and I will take possession of her. But if you respect my inclination, my wishes, my suffering; if you flatter my delusions, my hopes, then I will not oppose a recovery from them either, if it should present itself to me.

This last phrase flowed out of his pen, not out of his heart. Indeed, as he saw it on the paper, he began to cry bitterly. In one way or another he would have to renounce his happiness, yes, his unhappiness of loving Ottilie! For the first time now he was aware of what he was doing. He was departing without knowing what might come of it. At all events, he was not to see her again now; would he ever see her again, what assurance could he expect concerning that? But the letter was written. The horses stood before the door; each moment

                                                   KATHARINA MOMMSEN

caused him to fear he might catch sight of Ottilie somewhere and at the same time see his resolve brought to naught. He composed himself; he thought that it would still be possible for him to return at any moment and through his absence itself to come nearer to his desires. On the other hand he imagined Ottilie compelled to leave the house, if he stayed. He sealed the letter, hurried down the steps, and jumped on his horse . . .

(Part 1, Chapter 16)

Tragic Ending

. . . Nanny sees her lady grow pale and numb: she runs to Charlotte; they all come. The family friend who is a doctor hurries in; it appears to him to be only exhaustion. He has them bring some beef broth; Ottilie pushes it away with aversion; she even almost has convulsions when the cup is brought close to her mouth. He asks earnestly and with haste, as circumstances prompt him: What nourishment has Ottilie taken today? The girl hesitates; he repeats his question, the girl admits Ottilie has eaten nothing.

Nanny appears to him to be more uneasy than is reasonable. He pulls her into an adjacent room, Charlotte follows, the girl falls to her knees, she confesses that Ottilie has eaten as good as nothing for a long time. At Ottilie's insistence she has eaten the food in her stead; she has kept quiet about it, because of her mistress' pleading and threatening demeanor and also, she adds innocently, because it tasted so very good to her.

The Major and Mittler came in; they found Charlotte busy in the company of the doctor. The pale, ethereal child sat, still conscious, so it seemed, in the corner of the sofa. They ask her to lie down; she declines but indicates that they should pull up the little trunk. She puts her feet on it and lies in a comfortable, half-reclining position. She appears to be about to take her leave, her demeanor expresses to those around her the most tender affection, love, gratitude, regret, and the most heartfelt farewell.

Eduard, as he is dismounting, learns of the situation; he plunges into the room, throws himself down at her side, seizes her hand, and floods her with silent tears. He remains thus for a long time. Finally he cries out: "Shall I never hear your voice again? Will you not return to life with one word for me? Good, good! I'll follow you over, there we may speak in other tongues!"

She presses his hand forcefully, she looks at him with eyes full of life and love, and after drawing a deep breath, after a heavenly, silent motion of her lips: "Promise me to live!" she cries out with sweet and tender effort, but at once she sinks back.

"I promise!" he calls out to her, but he calls it only after her; for she has already departed.

After a tearful night it fell to Charlotte to take care of burying the loved one's remains. The Major and Mittler assisted her. Eduard's condition was deplorable. When he was just able to lift himself out of his despair and consider to some extent, he insisted that Ottilie should not be taken out of the castle; she should be waited on, cared for, treated as if she were alive; for she was not dead, she could not be dead. They did what he wanted, at least insofar as they did not do what he had forbidden. He did not demand to see her.

Still another frightful event struck, another worry occupied the friends. Nanny, severely reprimanded by the doctor, forced with threats to a confession, and after her confession overwhelmed with reproach, had run away. After a long search they found her again, she seemed beside herself. Her parents took her into their care. The best treatment did not seem to help, they had to confine her, because she threatened to run away again.

By degrees it was possible to rescue Eduard from his most intense despair but only to his distress; for it became clear to him that he had lost his life's happiness forever. They dared to explain to him that Ottilie, laid to rest in the chapel, would still remain among the living and not be deprived of a friendly, quiet dwelling place. It was hard to get his permission, and only on the condition that she be carried out in an open coffin and the vault be covered at most only with a glass cover, and that a lamp that burned perpetually be donated, did he at last consent to it and seemed to have acquiesced in everything.

They dressed the lovely body in the adornment she had prepared for herself; they put a wreath of asters on her head, which shone ominously like a sad constellation. To decorate the bier, the church, the chapel, all the gardens were divested of their ornaments. They lay desolate as if winter had already eradicated all joy from the beds. As early in the morning as possible she was carried out of the castle in an open coffin, and the rising sun put color in that heavenly face once more. Those escorting her pressed close around the bearers, no one wanted to go ahead, no one to follow, everyone wanted to encircle her, everyone wanted to enjoy her presence for the last time. Boys, men and women, no one remained unmoved. The young girls were disconsolate; they felt their loss most directly.

Nanny was missing. They had kept her away, or rather they had concealed from her the day and the hour of the burial. She was watched over by her parents in a room on the garden. But when she heard the bells toll, she was all too soon aware of what was happening; and when her attendant left her from curiosity to see the procession, she escaped out of a window into a passageway, and from there, because all the doors were locked, into the attic.

The procession was just moving hesitantly along through the village on the neat pathway strewn with petals. Nanny clearly saw her mistress among them, more distinct, more perfect, more beautiful than all those following the procession. Unworldly, as if borne by clouds or waves, she seemed to beckon to her servant; and the girl, confused, unsteady, reeling, plunged down.

The multitude scattered to all sides with a terrible cry. Because of the crowding and turmoil the bearers were forced to set the bier down. The child lay very close to it; all her limbs seemed to be shattered. They lifted her up; and by chance or by some special intervention they laid her across the body; in fact she herself seemed to want to reach her beloved lady with the last vestige of life. But scarcely had her trembling limbs touched Ottilie's garment, her powerless fingers touched Ottilie's folded hands, than the girl jumped up, first of all raised her arms and her eyes toward heaven, then threw herself down on her knees before the coffin and piously enraptured stared up at her mistress in wonder.

Finally she jumped up as if inspired and cried with sacred joy: "Yes, she has forgiven me! What no man, what I could not forgive myself, God forgives me through her glance, her gesture, her mouth. Now she is resting again so quiet and peaceful; but you saw how she sat up and blessed me with her unfolded hands, how she looked at me kindly! You heard it all, you are witnesses that she said to me: 'It is forgiven you!'—I am no longer a murderer among you; she has forgiven me, God has forgiven me, and no one can find fault with me anymore."

The crowd pressed close all around; they were astonished, they listened and looked this way and that, and no one knew exactly what to do. "Carry her to her rest now!" the girl said. "She has done and suffered her share and cannot live among us anymore." The bier moved on, Nanny was the first to follow it, and they reached the church, the chapel. . . .

Ottilie's continued beautiful condition, more like sleep than death, drew many people here. The local residents and neighbors wanted to look at her still; and each one wanted to hear the incredible story out of Nanny's mouth, some to scoff at it, most to have their doubts about it, but a few to conduct themselves as believers.

Every need whose real gratification is denied necessitates faith. Nanny, shattered before the eyes of the whole world, had become well again through the touch of this holy body; why should not a similar good fortune be given to others here? Loving mothers, at first secretly, brought their children who were afflicted by some sickness, and they believed they noticed a sudden improvement. The confidence increased, until at last no one was so old and so weak that he had not sought comfort and relief at this place. The throng grew, and they found it necessary to close the chapel, even the church, except for the hours of service.

Eduard did not dare to go see the dear departed again. He continued to live to himself alone; he seemed to have no more tears, to be capable of no more sorrow. His participation in the daily life around him, his enjoyment of food and drink, decreases every day. . . .

But from time to time an unrest steals over him. He longs to enjoy something again, he begins to talk again. "Oh," he said once to the Major, who scarcely left his side, "how unhappy I am that all of my endeavors remain only an imitation, a false effort! What has been bliss to her becomes agony to me; and still, for the sake of this bliss, I must take this agony upon myself. I must go after her, after her on this path; but my nature holds me back, and my promise. It is a terrible duty to imitate what cannot be imitated. I perceive well, dear friend, genius is needed for all things, even for martyrdom."

What shall we say, considering his hopeless condition, about the efforts to help of wife, friend, doctor, which those close to Eduard indulged in for a time. Finally they found him dead. Mittler was the first to make this sad discovery. He called the doctor and, with his usual composure, scrupulously examined the circumstances in which they had found the deceased. Charlotte came rushing

  KATHARINA MOMMSEN

in; she was animated by a suspicion of suicide; she was about to accuse herself, to accuse the others of unforgivable negligence. But the doctor was soon able to convince her of the contrary on the strength of natural causes and Mittler for moral reasons. Very clearly Eduard had been taken unaware by his end. Those things that before he used to conceal carefully, what was left to him of Ottilie in a quiet moment he had taken out of a little casket, out of a portfolio and spread them out before him: a lock of hair, flowers picked in a happy hour, all the small notes that she had written him from that first one that his wife had given him by chance, so full of presentiment. All of that he would not willingly have exposed to accidental discovery. And so this heart, too, so recently roused to constant turmoil, lay now impassively at rest; and since he had fallen asleep amidst thoughts of that holy one, so he might well be called blessed. Charlotte gave him his place next to Ottilie and ordered that no one else be interred in this vault. Along with this stipulation she made a handsome endowment to the church and school for the clergy and the teachers.

So the lovers rest next to each other. Peace hovers over their abode; serene, sympathetic angel figures look down on them from the arches; and what a friendly moment it will be when at some future time they awaken again together.

(Part 2, Chapter 18, end of the novel)

Conversation with Napoleon
on October 8, 1808, in Erfurt

Marshal Lannes and Minister Maret must have spoken favorably of me. The first had known me since 1806. A fat chamberlain, a Pole, told me to remain. The crowd withdrew. Presentation to Savary and Talleyrand. I am called in. At the same moment Daru sent in his name and was immediately admitted. For that reason, I hesitate. Am called again. Enter. The Emperor sits eating his breakfast at a great round table; at his right Talleyrand stands somewhat removed from the table, rather close at his left Daru, with whom he is talking about the matter of troop levies. The Emperor motions to me to approach. I stop at an appropriate distance before him. After he looked at me attentively, he said: "Vous êtes un homme. [You are a man.]" I bow.

He asks, "How old are you?"

"Sixty years."

"You are well preserved.—

"You have written tragedies."

I answered with what was necessary.

Here Daru began to speak. He had taken notice of German literature in order in some measure to flatter the Germans on whom he had to inflict so much misery, just as he was really very conversant in Latin and was himself an editor of Horace.

He conversed about me as perhaps my patrons in Berlin might have spoken; at least I recognized their way of thinking and their views in what he said.

Then he added that I had also translated from the French and, as a matter of fact, Voltaire's "Mahomet."

                                                      KATHARINA MOMMSEN

The Emperor rejoined: "That is not a good play," and explained in detail how out of place it was that the world conqueror gives such a disadvantageous portrayal of himself.

Then he turned the conversation to *Werther*, which he gave the impression he had studied through and through. After various quite accurate observations, he singled out a certain passage and said: "Why did you do that? It is not true to life"; something which he analyzed in detail and with absolute accuracy.

I listened to him with a cheerful face and answered with a pleased smile that in truth I did not know whether anyone had made the same criticism, but that I found it quite correct and admitted that in this passage something false might be identified. But I added that it could perhaps be forgiven the poet if he made use of a device that could not easily be detected to produce certain effects that he could not have achieved in a simple, natural way.

The Emperor seemed satisfied with that, turned back to the drama, and made very significant observations, like one who views the tragic theater with the greatest attention, just as a judge in the criminal court, and had at the same time felt very deeply the departure of the French theater from nature and truth.

And so he came to the fate tragedies that he objected to. They should have belonged to a darker time. "What," he said, "do they want with fate now, politics is fate."

He turned back to Daru then and spoke with him about the great matter of troop levies; I stepped back a bit and happened to be standing in the alcove where more than thirty years before among many happy hours I had also passed many cheerless ones, and I had time to notice that to my right, toward the entrance doors, Berthier, Savary, and someone else, too, were standing. Talleyrand had departed.

Marshal Soult was announced. This large figure with a very thick head of hair entered. The Emperor asked jovially about some unpleasant events in Poland, and I had time to look around me in the room and remember the past. Here, too, there were the old carpets. But the portraits on the walls had disappeared. Here had hung the picture of the Duchess Amalie in fancy-dress costume, a black half-mask in her hand; the other likenesses of officials and family members were all missing.

The Emperor stood up, charged towards me, and with a type of maneuver cut me off from the ranks of the others in which I stood.

While he had his back turned toward them and spoke to me in a moderate voice, he asked whether I was married, had children, and all those personal matters that are customarily of interest. As well as also about my relations with the royal house, about Duchess Amalie, the Duke, the Duchess, and others; I answered him in a natural way. He seemed satisfied and translated this himself into his own language, only in a somewhat more peremptory way than I could have expressed myself.

At the same time I must note in general that during the whole conversation I had to admire the diversity of his expressions of approval, for he seldom listened impassively: either he nodded his head reflectively or said "oui" or even "c'est bien," or the like; also I should not forget to remark that whenever he had spoken, he generally added:

"Qu'en dit Mr. Göt."

And so I took an opportunity to inquire of the chamberlain with a gesture, if I might withdraw, which he reciprocated, and I then took my leave without more ado.

What Is Important in Life

Montan, motivated by some of Wilhelm's contradictions, explained himself further: "If one finally knows what really matters, then one ceases to be talkative." "Well, then, what really matters?" Wilhelm replied abruptly. "That can easily be said," the former replied: "To think and to do, to do and to think, that is the sum of all wisdom, recognized from time immemorial, practiced from time immemorial, not understood by everyone. The two must move constantly to and fro in life, like breathing in and out; like question and answer the one should not take place without the other. One who makes a law for himself of what the spirit of human understanding secretly whispers in the ear of each newborn babe—to test action with thought, thought with action—he cannot err, and if he errs, he will soon find his way back to the right path."

(*Wilhelm Meister's Journeyman Years*
Book 2, Chapter 9)

The Main Theme of World History and Human History

The real, single, and innermost theme of world history and the history of mankind, to which all others are subordinated, remains the conflict of skepticism and faith. All epochs in which faith prevails, in whatever shapes it may choose, are brilliant, heart stirring, and productive for contemporary times and for coming generations. On the other hand, all epochs in which skepticism, in whatever form it may appear, asserts a pitiful victory, and even though they should boast of the appearance of splendor, will vanish for future ages, because no one enjoys toiling over the realization of what is unproductive.

(*Notes and Essays Concerning the* West-East Divan
Chapter: "Israel in the Desert.")

 KATHARINA MOMMSEN

From the *West-East Divan* (1819)

God is of the east possessed,
God is ruler of the west;
North and south alike, each land
Rests within His gentle hand.

Translated by E.A. Bowring
(Moganni Nameh, Book of the Minstrel.
Talismans)

The twofold blessing in respiration:
The air drawn in and its exhalation;
One sets it free, one bids it stay;
So life is mixed in this wonderful way.
Give thanks to God for pressing you so,
And thank Him when He again lets you go.

Blessed Longing

Tell it only to the wise,
For the crowd at once will jeer:
That which is alive I praise,
That which longs for death by fire.

Cooled by passionate love at night,
Procreated, procreating,
You have known the alien feeling
In the calm of candlelight;

Gloom-embraced will lie no more,
By the flickering shades obscured,
But are seized by new desire,
To a higher union lured.

Then no distance holds you fast;
Winged, enchanted, on you fly,
Light your longing, and at last,
Moth, you meet the flame and die.

Never prompted to that quest:
Die and dare rebirth!
You remain a dreary quest
On our gloomy earth.

Translated by Michael Hamburger

KATHARINA MOMMSEN

Book of Love

Strangest book of all the books
Is the book of love;
Attentively I have read it:
Seldom words of gladness,
Many leaves of sorrow;
One whole section talks of parting.
A reunion! one small chapter,
But a fragment. Tomes of grief
Lengthened by great explanations,
Endless, measureless.
O Nisami!—at the ending
You have found the proper pathway;
The unsolvable, who solves it?
Lovers finding one another.

What makes time short to me?
    Activity!
What makes it long and spiritless?
    'Tis idleness!
What brings us to debt?
    To delay and forget!
What makes us succeed?
    Decisions with speed!
How to fame to ascend?
    Oneself to defend!

Translated by E.A. Bowring

Foolish it is that each one should cherish
In every case his separate thought!
If God's devotion by *Islam* is taught,
In Islam all of us live and we perish.

He who knows man's true intent
Here will have decided:
Orient and Occident
Cannot be divided.

So between worlds ever staying,
Thoughtfully one's choices weighing,
Best both East and West sustaining,
In between the two remaining.

KATHARINA MOMMSEN

Poems from the Later Years

"The greatest men, whom I have known and who had an open prospect over heaven and earth, were humble men and knew how to value things in stages."
(Goethe to Lavater, June 24, 1780)

Humility

The masters' works I look upon,
And I can see what they have done;
When looking upon this or that by me,
What I should have done is what I see.

(1815)
Translated by
Christopher Middleton

Were not the eye so like the sun,
The sun's rays it could never capture;
Were not the strength in us God's own,
How could the godlike bring us rapture!

(1805/1810)

Johann Wolfgang von Goethe. Oil painting by Joseph K. Stieler, 1828.

KATHARINA MOMMSEN

When in the infinite repeated
What is the same flows ever on,
And thousandfold the arch, completed,
Is in itself with power drawn,
Then lust for life from all things surges,
From all the stars with one accord,
And all our striving then emerges
As endless peace in God, the Lord.

(1827)

Primeval Words, Orphic

Daimon

As on the day in which your life began
The sun to stars and planets was related,
So you unfolded, following a plan
Determined on the day you were created.
Thus you must be, escape you never can,
Sibyls and prophets long ago thus stated.
And neither time nor force can ever break
The finished form that growing life will take.

Chance

These strict confines are softly bypassed, though,
By change that changes with us as we stride.
You do not stay alone; with friends you come and go,
You act indeed like others by your side.
Life brings adjustment, motion to and fro—
It is an idle ride, and so you ride.
Soon year and year in rounding chain combine,
The lamp awaits the spar, to make it shine.

Love

And it will come! Down from the sky he flings
Himself, to which from earthly dust he rose.
He floats along upon his airy wings;
Around his head and chest a spring day flows.
He seems to flee, then back from flight he swings,
While bliss from pain, or joy from anguish, grows.
The hearts of many men may hither float, or yon;
The noblest heart, however, stays with one.

Necessity

There 'tis again—the planets' whim, anew:
All regulations, laws, and every will
Are only willed as something we must do.
Where will prevails, caprice must come to nil;
Your heart's desires shall be withheld from you,
And that which Must commands, Will must fulfill.
Thus freedom—an illusion of the heart—
Has, after years, more limits than at start.

Hope

The gate, though, in this wall of limitation,
Shall soon be opened up—that hateful gate!
Let it but stand upon its firm foundation!
A spirit rises from it, free and straight.
She lifts us on her wings to liberation;
From clouds and mist toward a better fate.
Familiar is her flight, and to no land confined;
One stroke of wings—and eons lie behind!

(1817)
Translated by
Max Knight and Joseph Fabry

KATHARINA MOMMSEN

The Lookout's Song

My talent is seeing,
To look is my task,
The tower my being,
The world all I ask.
Far off I am gazing,
I see what is near,
The heavens amazing,
The woods and the deer.
Adornment forever
I see, through and through,
As it gives me pleasure,
I please myself, too.
How happy my eye is
To see it; whate'er
The how or the why is,
It was still so fair.

(*Faust II*, Act 5. Deep Night. Lynceus, the Lookout, on the
castle watch tower, singing. 1831)

Political Poems from the Later Period

Wanderer's Song
(before emigrating to America)

All the mountainside surrounding,
Down the hills and dales along,
There's the sound of wings resounding,
There all's movement as in song;
Unconditional the force now
That to joy and counsel leads;
May your aim come from love's source now
And your life be in your deeds.

For my fetters I now sever
And my trustfulness is gone;
Can I say what new endeavor
Or what chance I'll happen on
As I leave now, as I wander,
Like a widow full of woe,
With some other over yonder
Ever onward I must go!

In this land no more remaining,
Venture boldly, go and roam!
Strength in head and arm sustaining,
Everywhere they are at home;
Where the sun is always by us,

KATHARINA MOMMSEN

There our every care is past;
'Neath it wandering we'll hie us,
Therefore is the world so vast.
(from Wilhelm Meister's Journeyman Years, 1821)

Today and Always

No one can show another day to that day,
Bewildered in bewilderment reflected,
But each one feels it right and proper his way,
Restricting others, he is unrestricted;
'Tis better if his sealed lips have no say,
His mind meanwhile as if on wings convected.
Today comes not from yesterday; past ages,
In turn, will fall, then reign, on history's pages.

(1819)

National Assembly

On the left and on the right wing,
Radicals and in the middle,
Sitting, standing up and fighting,
Each one is the other's riddle.

When you give your whole endeavor,
And you vote as you've a mind to,
Mark the ties you now will sever,
Sense the ones that this will find you.

(1820)

Goethe dictates to the scribe, John, in his study. Oil painting by J.J. Schmeller, 1831.

KATHARINA MOMMSEN

A Citizen's Duty

If every one will *sweep* his street,
Then every city quarter's neat.
If every one will *do* his lesson,
Then it'll go well in the council session.

(1832, shortly before Goethe's death)

He is the most fortunate of men who can associate the end of his life with its beginning.

(*Maxims and Reflections*, 1821)

Charitable to the last day of his life (March 22, 1832). Goethe's doctor gives an account of the dying poet:

Since the demise of his only son and since the lung hemorrhage that brought him so near death's door a few weeks later, Goethe had often made quiet mention to me of his end as not far distant anymore and especially had several times taken the occasion to commend to me those institutions that he cared for and also particularly individuals employed in them, for whom "I could be efficacious with them longer, after all, than he." In the course of the conversation of that day [probably the ninth of March], he returned to this matter and again shared with me his intentions, plans, and hopes with reference to this matter, with coherence and in detail. Anyone who had heard him then, as well as on earlier similar occasions when his acts containing abundant evidence were open to view, anyone who, in short, like me, had been an agent of so many charitable deeds that Goethe granted in secret on his own initiative and from his own means to those needing help, especially the sick, would not doubt that the reproach, as frequent as it was unkind, that the deceased had troubled himself about the weal and woe of others, namely, even his subordinates, at best from gross egotism, could have been devised only by insolent, malicious slander or by the most avaricious effrontery. Certainly, common begging and charity coerced without merit were offensive to him in the highest degree, and—at all times perhaps too unconditionally desirous of secrecy as the result of unpleasant experiences—he liked to avoid any ostentation in the distribution of his benefactions.

Happy that he had come through a sickness, neither of us in that moment suspected that Goethe really had just set forth his last official wishes. Still, after this communication he performed only one more half-involuntary official function, in that on the twentieth of March, two days before he passed away, without my knowledge he signed with a trembling hand the order for payment of a subsidy to a talented young woman from Weimar [Angelika Facius] pursuing her artistic training abroad, for whom he had always provided like a father. With this he wrote his name for the last time.

(Carl Vogel, The Last Sickness of Goethe)